"Is there comfort when there are no answers to life's tragedies and losses? *Lifting Our Eyes* answers that question with a resounding, 'Yes!'"

—Don Piper, coauthor of *90 Minutes in Heaven* and
Heaven Is Real

"While we wish it were not so, lovely and innocent people sometimes fall into the path of sickness and evil. Where is God? He's in the aftermath, illuminating the character of the lost, the grace of survivors, and the purpose behind the senseless. God is big, and this book will show you how big he is."

—Leslie Haskin, 9/11 survivor and author of
Between Heaven and Ground Zero and *Held*

"*Lifting Our Eyes* introduces us to some remarkable VA Tech staff and students. Beth Lueders describes how some lived through those dark days of tragedy, as well as the legacy of some who died in the massacre. I'm so moved by the story of how these Campus Crusade students demonstrated their faith in both life and death."

—Mark Gauthier, U.S. campus director,
Campus Crusade for Christ

LIFTING OUR EYES

Finding God's Grace
Through the Virigina Tech Tragedy
The Lauren McCain Story

BETH J. LUEDERS

BERKLEY BOOKS, NEW YORK

THE BERKLEY PUBLISHING GROUP
Published by the Penguin Group
Penguin Group (USA) Inc.
375 Hudson Street, New York, New York 10014, USA
Penguin Group (Canada), 90 Eglinton Avenue East, Suite 700, Toronto, Ontario M4P 2Y3, Canada
(a division of Pearson Penguin Canada Inc.)
Penguin Books Ltd., 80 Strand, London WC2R 0RL, England
Penguin Group Ireland, 25 St. Stephen's Green, Dublin 2, Ireland (a division of Penguin Books Ltd.)
Penguin Group (Australia), 250 Camberwell Road, Camberwell, Victoria 3124, Australia
(a division of Pearson Australia Group Pty. Ltd.)
Penguin Books India Pvt. Ltd., 11 Community Centre, Panchsheel Park, New Delhi—110 017, India
Penguin Group (NZ), 67 Apollo Drive, Rosedale, North Shore 0745, Auckland, New Zealand
(a division of Pearson New Zealand Ltd.)
Penguin Books (South Africa) (Pty.) Ltd., 24 Sturdee Avenue, Rosebank, Johannesburg 2196,
South Africa

Penguin Books Ltd., Registered Offices: 80 Strand, London WC2R 0RL, England

LIFTING OUR EYES

This book is an original publication of The Berkley Publishing Group.

Please refer to pages v–vi for a complete listing of the versions of the Bible that have been used within this book for Scripture quotations.

PRINTING HISTORY
Berkley trade paperback edition / September 2007

Berkley trade paperback ISBN: 978-0-425-22113-6

An application to register this book for cataloging has been submitted to the Library of Congress.

PRINTED IN THE UNITED STATES OF AMERICA

10 9 8 7 6 5 4 3 2 1

Most Berkley Books are available at special quantity discounts for bulk purchases for sales promotions, premiums, fund-raising, or educational use. Special books, or book excerpts, can also be created to fit specific needs.

For details, write: Special Markets, The Berkley Publishing Group, 375 Hudson Street, New York, New York 10014.

SCRIPTURE REFERENCES

*To the Virginia Tech students and professors
who lost their lives and to the world of loved ones
who lift up your legacies*

ACKNOWLEDGMENTS

Soli Deo Gloria! Without divine inspiration and strength from my Sustainer, you would not being reading these words. *Lifting Our Eyes* is not about the people featured in each chapter, or about me—this book is truly about God loving us so much to bring abundant life from the heaviness of death.

A most fervent thanks to those who carried me through the grueling research and writing of this book. Your unfailing love and support never ceases to amaze me. If I listed each of you by name, I'd have to write another book! But special kudos go to my dedicated cadre of friends (Angie, Blythe, Chris, Daria, Jules, Karen, Kathy, Kristi, Laura, Lisa, and Terry), who relentlessly believe in me and who faithfully administer pep talks, hugs, prayers, and chocolate. You keep me lighthearted and grateful with each new day. Ann, Diane, Helen, Laura, and Shelly, your professionalism saved the day. Thank you! And my most treasured prayer team and Bible Babes—you motivate me to keep seeking the things above.

I also lift my heart in tearful appreciation to my parents, who paved the way for me to study journalism in college and who are now reading this book from heaven. Bless you for encouraging me to follow my dreams. To my agent, Greg; editor, Denise; and the team at Berkley, thank you for taking a chance on such a whirlwind adventure.

I also extend a special thanks to each generous soul in this book, especially Dave and Sherry McCain, who willingly shared their bittersweet stories of both sorrow and joy. On behalf of the readers, we honor you, we stand with you in your personal journeys of grief and remembrance. May you continue to experience God's grace and peace with each new day.

P.S. Lauren, because of your brave faith, your quirky humor, and your infectious love for people, I write this note to you:

On my drive away from your campus, I pull off Exit 191 at a petite rest stop overflowing with retirees just unloading from a tour bus. My heart sinks at the sight of the fifty gabbing women waddling their way to the one already crammed potty room. *Lord, have mercy!*

Next door, I eye the men's room with only a trickle of white-haired users. *Nah!* I peel out for the next rest stop, but later smile and think of you. I just bet you would've grabbed a friend's hand and headed straight for the guys' room. I can't wait to meet you where there will be no more lines for the ladies' room.

CONTENTS

Foreword by Darrell Scott   *xv*

Author's Reflections   *xvii*

Chapter 1   NO WORDS   *1*

Chapter 2   "PLEASE CALL."   *23*

Chapter 3   LIGHTS IN THE DARKNESS   *45*

Chapter 4   THE LOVE OF MY LIFE   *63*

Chapter 5   "THIS STINKS. THIS HURTS."   *81*

Chapter 6   I CAN ONLY IMAGINE   *101*

Chapter 7   HOPE FOR THE HELPLESS   *119*

Chapter 8   I FORGIVE YOU   *133*

Chapter 9   CIRCLE OF FRIENDS   *149*

Chapter 10   DANCING BEFORE HIM   *165*

A Letter from Sherry McCain   *179*

In Memoriam   *185*

Contents

Where Is God in the Midst of Tragedy?   *201*

Tears and Fears   *213*

Notes   *241*

FOREWORD

Life is unpredictable. Some of us will live to be one hundred and others will die at the age of seven or seventeen, like my daughter, Rachel Scott. She was the first to be killed in the Columbine shootings in 1999. It's not the quantity of time we spend here, but the quality of life that matters.

Rachel's life counted. Her story has touched the lives of millions of people around the world since the Columbine tragedy. Lauren McCain's life, and the lives of the other innocent people who were massacred at Virginia Tech, will count as well. This book compels us to face the fact that life is short, and all of us must make the most of the time we have.

A mentor in my life taught me to "see through" the circumstances of life rather than "look at" them. Many will view Virginia Tech's tragedy the same way they viewed Columbine's: as a tragedy with no redeeming side to it. Others will "see through" the tragedy and learn incredible lessons from it as well as from the lives of those who died that day.

One of the darkest days in human history was the day Jesus was crucified, and yet Christians view it as the day of redemption for the world. May these stories inspire you and challenge you to live life to the fullest.

—Darrell Scott, father of Rachel Scott,
Columbine's first victim

AUTHOR'S REFLECTIONS

I used to roll my eyes when my journalism professor directed our class to write another obituary. I thought to myself, *Whatever. How boring, how mundane. Is this what it means to be a writer?* Today I wrote thirty-two obituaries, and instead of rolling my eyes, I dabbed at them with a tissue.

If we forego our cocksure attitudes, time has a mysterious way of teaching us about the foundational essentials of life: No one is immune from suffering. People we cherish do die. But the Ruler of the universe is still in control and does fashion good from life's bad.

April 18, 2007, two days after America's deadliest gunfire massacre mars the Virginia Tech campus in Blacksburg, Virginia, I read an e-mail that several students involved with Campus Crusade for Christ at the school were killed in the shootings or eyewitnesses to the chaos. Involved with this ministry in my own college days, and then later as a full-time media staff person, I feel a special tug in my heart. I drop to my knees in prayer, sensing God say, "This story does not end with these deaths. Seung-Hui Cho will *not* have the last say. I want *my* story told."

The next week I fly to Virginia feeling a bit like Abraham who, according to Hebrews 11:8 (NIV), ". . . obeyed and went, even though he did not know where he was going." I had visited Virginia before, but never in a dinky rental car driving nearly five hours alone through unknown rolling mountains . . . at night. But with God as my tour guide, I settle in for the ride.

I never thought while sitting in college journalism classes that almost thirty years later I would be back on a university campus applying what my J-school professors instilled in me. Observe. Question. Listen. Report.

Taking my first steps on the sprawling Blue Ridge campus, my instincts kick in as a world-traveled journalist, but my heart knows better. Despite my professional training to get the story at all costs, I heed the voice of someone more astute than my media instructors.

I choose to tune in to the voice of my Creater, the one who nudges me to show up in Blacksburg in the first place. I do, and what you are about to read is only part of God's unfolding story through the terrifying events at Virginia Tech. His handiwork of weaving grace throughout the tattered shreds of evil is long from reaching the final stitch.

During my two trips to Blacksburg, within the first month of the shootings, I trace the likely steps of Cho that fateful Monday morning. I walk to West Ambler Johnston Hall, then north across the Drillfield, and up the steps to Norris Hall. Several times I visit the North Main Post Office, less than a block from campus, where Cho mailed his manifesto package. My skin shivers a little every time I pick up my own overnight-mail envelope inside the old-fashioned brick building. I'd stand in line and wonder, *What was Cho thinking when he filled in the mailing label to send his rage-filled last words to the world? Did he use this same post-office pen?*

I also drive to the local Wal-Mart in Christiansburg and meander around the hunting and ammunitions section, with real-life stuffed turkey, bobcat, and fish on display. For most folks in rural Virginia, bullets are for hunting these and other animals, not humans. My stomach clenches when I peer at the gun case stocked with gun shells and bullets. Cho allegedly stood here, too, stocking up on his deadly rounds.

I also visit the memorial stones on the rim of the Drill-field and read tender notes left to the killed students and professors. Seeing these temporary "gravestones" piled with flowers and good-bye poems reminds me of my visit to the Columbine memorials shortly after the 1999 high-school shootings. In both Littleton and Blacksburg, I am taken aback by personal letters extending forgiveness to the student killers.

Through dozens of conversations with Virginia Tech family members, survivors, students, professors, and community members, I catch glimpses of God's grace and goodness amid the unimaginable brokenness and pain.

God's grace continues to spread gently across Hokie central. The professor who organizes a team to handle yard work for his colleague's grieving widow. The families who open their homes and arms to weary students needing respite. The pastors and counselors who listen and console. The friends who hold each other through their agonizing wails.

As I drive away from Virginia Tech on April 27, I hear a song on the radio based on the words of Psalm 121:1–2. With one hand on the wheel, I scribble these words in a paisley notebook a friend gave me just for my trip: "Lifting Our Eyes."

It is my prayer that each chapter of this book encourages you to lift your eyes from your own unsettling times of fear, loss, and hurt to the gracious and glorious Maker of heaven and Earth, our ever-present Helper.

CHAPTER ONE
NO WORDS

He was shooting people as he saw them.
It was so loud. But he never said
a word the whole time.

—TREY PERKINS, VIRGINIA TECH SOPHOMORE

Subfreezing northwest winds howl across the Virginia Polytechnic Institute and State University campus in the early hours of Monday, April 16. Window screens rattle, tree branches dip and sway, loose trash whooshes into bushes. The wintry winds and ominous skies invading Blacksburg, Virginia, mean business.

So does a senior English major living in 2121 Harper Hall just east of West Campus Drive, one dormitory removed from West Ambler Johnston Hall (West AJ).

Close to 4:20 A.M., the bone-chilling weather conditions whip up flurries of snow. Inside West AJ, exhausted freshman Molly Donohue returns to her fourth floor room from the lounge where she's been studying all night with

3

her boyfriend. Molly sets her alarm for 6:50 and stumbles into bed. The petite redhead doses off about 4:30.

A half hour later in his Harper dorm suite, Seung-Hui Cho brushes past his suitemate in their bathroom. Blank-faced Cho gives his usual greeting—no words, just an expressionless turn-away. The South Korean born Cho brushes his teeth and dabs acne cream on his stern face. Cho already knows what he will wear that day.

Two hours later Cho and Molly's worlds collide in West AJ.

I usually always hear my alarm and immediately shut it off. But on Monday morning with only two and half hours of sleep, I turn my alarm off and stay in bed half awake. All of a sudden I hear a scream. The sound shocks me awake, but because I'm still drowsy, I wonder if I do hear a scream.

I roll out of bed and look at my clock—it's 7:15 A.M. and I'm late to meet my boyfriend for breakfast. I pull on my jeans and shoes when I hear pounding followed by a very, very strange scream. The scream comes from my girlfriends' room next door. Our walls are pretty thin.

I hear more pounding and my roommate wakes up and sees me standing in the middle of the room.

I run to our door, but pause . . . I hear a door slam loudly. Next I hear running down the hall and past my room. I open my door and I see blood on the floor and sneaker prints of blood. The bloody prints are right outside my room!

I don't know what to think. The pounding sounded like a loft bed falling apart, and I assume the girls next door have one and someone just fell out. When I see the bloody sneaker prints I think to myself, *Should I follow these sneaker prints to see if that's the person who's hurt, and that's why he's running?* Then I think, *Oh, I bet it's Emily's roommate running to get help.* I go to Emily and Heather's room and I try to open the door—but there is a man's body pressed up against the door. I see his arm in the doorway.

I yell, "Is everything all right? Is everything all right?" I look up toward the bed, but I can't see anyone. The room is dark and there's this man against the door. All of a sudden I think to myself, *Wait. Is this an intruder?* I'm scared and run to my RA's room— but he isn't there. His door is wide open. I run back to my room and tell my roommate, "I can't find Ryan. Something is terribly wrong. Something terrible has happened." My roommate suggests we get our female RA and leaves to find her.

I finish dressing quickly and meet my roommate, two girls in a neighboring room, and the RA in the hallway. We all stand there for a few seconds, afraid to move past my room. The RA approaches Emily's room and busts through the door. Seconds later the RA comes out with complete horror on her face. We start questioning her and she's not hearing us. She just keeps repeating. "I need a phone. I need a phone."

Horrifying fear clenches Molly's heart. In a swirl of panic, the female resident advisor discovers the bodies of Emily and Stack, each with gunshot wounds to the head. The RA calls 911. Stack dies at the scene. An ambulance rushes Emily to Montgomery Regional Hospital in Blacksburg.

With the bitter winds gusting near 55 mph, no rescue helicopter can assist. Paramedics speed the wounded freshman to the closest level-one trauma center in Roanoke, approximately twenty-five miles away. Emily dies en route.

"I mostly think about [Emily's] scream," recalls a traumatized Molly two days later on *Good Morning America*. "I don't necessarily hear it, but I remember how I felt when I heard it." The morning of April 16, 2007, felt anything but good to Molly and everyone affected by murderous actions of the deeply disturbed twenty-three-year-old senior, Seung-Hui Cho.

While investigators descend on West AJ that morning, concluding that the double shooting was an isolated event, university officials make a fateful decision. They calculate that there is no immediate need to lock down the twenty-six-thousand-acre Virginia Tech campus.

After his first strike in West AJ, Cho returns to his dorm room and gathers his multimedia arsenal—an eighteen-hundred-word rambling tirade, twenty-eight video and audio clips, and forty-three still photographs. At 9:01 A.M., the troubled senior overnights a package to NBC News in New York City—using the wrong ZIP code, which delays delivery by one day.

On the mail receipt, Cho lists himself as "A. Ishmael," perhaps in reference to Abraham's firstborn son through Sarah's concubine. The Bible's Genesis 16:12 declares this about ancient Ishmael: "He will be a wild donkey of a man; his hand will be against everyone and everyone's hand against him, and he will live in hostility toward all his brothers" (NIV).

One can't help but catch the creepy symbolism of "wild donkey" Cho, who was alienated against everyone and whose final moments on Earth hurl him into "hostility toward all his brothers."

In his self-compiled obituary, Cho seethes about the "Christian Criminals" who shamed, raped, and crucified him and other "Weak and Defenseless." He rails against wealthy "brats" and "snobs." The antisocial collegiate compares himself to Jesus Christ and applauds the 1999 Columbine High School killers. (Cho's murderous spree fell four days before the eighth anniversary of the Colorado massacre.) Cho's rancid diatribe, punctuated with foul language and twisted reasoning, reveals the depth of his misguided soul.

"You had a hundred billion chances and ways to have avoided today. But you decided to spill my blood. You forced me into a corner and gave me only one option. The decision was yours," Cho vents in one of his passages. "Now you have blood on your hands that will never wash off. . . . I didn't have to do this. I could have left. I could have fled. But no, I will no longer run."

Seemingly on the run with his own personal demons, Cho includes a montage of unsettling photos with his manifesto. Garbed in a black T-shirt, black gloves, and a tan military-style vest with plenty of pockets for ammunition, the mean-faced loner leaves behind a photographic threat. In one photo he puts a knife to his throat; in another he jams a handgun against his own close-cropped head, just above his right ear. One of the most disturbing photos brings viewers up close to the looming barrel of his handgun.

The twenty-three-year-old last modifies his manifesto PDF files at 7:24 A.M., then waits for his brutal monologue on the world's stage. He mails his hate-filled package in Blacksburg's main post office just a few blocks from campus. Fueled with fresh adrenaline and cruel calculation, Cho turns his focus toward Norris Hall, home of the school's engineering and mathematics departments.

At 9:26, Virginia Tech administration distributes a campus-wide e-mail.

A shooting occurred at West Ambler Johnston earlier this morning. Police are on the scene and are investigating. The university community is urged to be cautious and are asked to contact Virginia Tech Police if you observe anything suspicious or with information on the case.... We will post as soon as we have more information.

Within minutes of this innocuous posting, Cho annihilates the sense of safety and security taken for granted by most American college students. At approximately 9:30, Cho marches into Norris Hall and chains shut several entry/exit doors before unleashing his last-stand rampage on the building's second floor.

Haiyan Cheng, a Virginia Tech computer science Ph.D. candidate recalls:

Boom. Boom. Boom. The horrible-sounding gunshots fire repeatedly. All I can do is kneel behind the lecture podium and pray to God, "Please stop him! Please stop the gunfire! Please . . ."

I'm teaching CS4414—Issues in Scientific Computing to senior students in the school of engineering that morning in Norris Hall 205. My advisor is out of town at a conference, and as a research and teaching assistant, I step in to teach his 9:05 class. Our second-floor classroom is the first on the left as you enter from the south stairs. On my way to class I see a white-haired professor in Room 204 across the hall taking notes out of his briefcase.

About 9:40, with some fifteen minutes left to the lecture, I turn my discussion to the numerical solution of ODEs, ordinary differential equations. I'm writing on the blackboard when suddenly a loud *bang, bang, bang,* interrupts me.

The thunderous sounds seem close—like some kind of construction noise. The banging stops for about ten seconds. I'm about to start on the topic of stability analysis when the disturbing noise starts again. A female student in the front row close to the door gets up to investigate. I follow her with lecture notes in my hand.

The door is always wide open during lectures, so both of us just stick our heads into the hallway. We hear the banging from Room 206, across the hall to the left of our classroom. I just stand there gazing at the closed 206 door.

In a flash, a guy walks out holding a black handgun. I am shocked! I only see him for a quick second or two, but his face is roundish and he's wearing black.

The student and I duck back inside and immediately shut the door. Instantly gunfire explodes in the hallway; the vibration hurts my ears. I shout to the class, "He has a gun in his hand! He has a gun in his hand! Everybody get down!" The female student and I duck behind the podium and a male student joins us. I squeeze his hoodie jacket so tight—as if holding my whole life there.

He looks into my eyes and I look into his. Both of us are numb with shock. Other students get down under tables. One male student just sits dazed in his chair, but then shouts, "We should block the door so he can't come in!"

The male student hiding next to me quickly runs to help three other guys in the class push a big table near the podium sideways against the door. The door has no window or lock.

The four male students stay on their stomachs holding the table's legs with their hands. We had two bomb threats the week before, but I have no idea how serious this present situation will become. We continue to hear rapid gunshots firing in the hallway. Next, the shooter moves to our classroom.

The gunman powerfully shoulders the door trying to force his way in. He shoves the door open about five inches. My students strain really hard against the propped table. Immediately the gunman fires two shots high into the door as if to hit someone in the chest. Wood chips and metal pieces fly everywhere. One bullet hits the podium where the female student and I hide.

Two of my students at the back of the room lying between the desks call 911 with their cell phones. I hear them quietly talking to the police about the gunman and our location in Room 205. Outside our room we hear clicking sounds. The shooter is reloading his gun.

A clip drops to the floor. We all tense up thinking he will attack our door again with more force and more bullets. But the shooter finally gives up and moves down the hallway.

I stay kneeling, praying softly out loud to God to stop the gunfire coming from other classrooms. The *bang, bang, bang,* just keeps repeating. We listen to at least another forty shots or so go off farther and farther down the hall. It is terrible.

We hear police sirens outside. The gunfire continues to boom. My students and I remain frozen in our positions on the floor. We wait . . . and wait.

One student asks if we should all jump out the window since we know the police are outside. We are only on the second floor, but we all agree that we should just stay inside. A few people walk around and try to comfort the others who are most visibly upset.

All the students gather near me at the front of the room. One student calls her mom to tell her of our scary situation. We wait . . . and wait. After a number of stressful minutes we hear someone shout outside our door, "Show me your hands, show me your hands." We are not sure if this is the police. Finally someone knocks on our door. The guys make sure it is the police before we open the door.

A policeman with a gun in his hand orders us to put up our hands and move to the back of the classroom. He is extremely cautious, as if one of us could be the gunman. He asks if anyone is injured. We gratefully tell him, "There's no gunman here. Nobody is injured." He directs us to sit down and stay calm. (As if that is easy to do.)

The policeman starts to leave and one student asks the officer to close the door. We fear the gunman is still loose and will return to our classroom. The officer assures us that we are safe and calls another police officer to stay with us.

This policeman instructs us to leave behind our personal things, form a line, and run after him. I see the emptied gun clip on the floor right outside of our classroom. We run quickly and try not to step in the blood on the floor. I just keep looking at my feet, running as fast as I can.

One student running right behind me starts to cry. She see bodies in the classrooms and begins shaking. I turn around and hold her hand. Together we rush out of the building. We dart behind Norris to Randolph Hall.

I am literally shaking when we run into Randolph. We gather in a classroom and a secretary brings us water. I borrow one of my students' cell phone to notify my husband, but I can't get through. I borrow a laptop from another student and e-mail my husband and my research group, telling them I am safe.

I am so proud of all my students. They did a great job in helping save our lives. I am so sorry about the students and professors who died. A few minutes before class I saw many of these people sitting in their classrooms—within the hour they were dead. The thought keeps coming to me: *What if the killer had tried our door first?* I actually think he did walk past our door before he went to Room 207 right next door.

Life is just so fragile. We have no control over it. I know it's going to take a long time to recover from this. The "whys" are difficult for everyone. I've found lots of comfort and support from my church and my family and friends.

The shootings have reminded me that we all need to cherish every minute of our lives. I think there is a reason God spared my life and my students' lives, but I don't know why. I think only he knows.

In nine rapid-fire minutes, cold-blooded Cho rains down death in this mountain town of about forty thousand. Cho releases his most potent venom on the second floor of Norris Hall, where reportedly, he was taking a second-semester sociology class called Deviant Behavior. The irony is sobering.

In Norris 206, where Haiyan Cheng sees the shooter emerge, Cho charges into round two of his killing spree. Bullets spew in Professor G. V. Loganathan's advanced hydrology class. Students scatter for cover. A bullet strikes an Indonesian doctoral student and his lifeless body collapses on a fellow graduate student. The dead student's body shields his classmate from lethal wounds.

Jarrett Lane, a civil engineering senior, was granted special permission to take Loganathan's graduate-level class. Both Lane and Loganathan are among ten slain during Cho's wordless slaughter in Room 206. Only four students survive.

Like a mobster hunting down a snitch, Cho methodically squeezes the trigger of his pistols, a .22-caliber Walther P22 and a 9mm Glock 19. Callous. Stone-faced. Surging with unrelenting adrenaline, Cho guarantees his actions speak louder than words. For what seems like an eternity, he zigzags into classrooms, returning to many rooms to finish off any wounded stragglers.

Romanian-born Holocaust survivor Liviu Librescu braces his body against the door of Room 204 while urging his students to kick out window screens and jump to safety. Most of the students escape alive, their seventy-six-year-old hero does not.

Cho's first bullet in Room 207 slices into the head of

thirty-five-year-old Jamie Bishop, known as Herr Bishop to his German-class students. Holding guns in both hands, the silent intruder picks off students like decoy ducks at an amusement park.

At the front of the class sits Lauren McCain, who told her freshman orientation class last summer, "I want everyone to know I love Jesus!" Cries, shouts, and moans echo loudly in the blood-smeared room. Someone vomits. Cruel-hearted Cho turns and leaves after a minute and a half.

Three classmates run to the door and slam their feet against it to keep Cho out in case he returns for more methodic murder. Soon the madman does return and the three students strain with their arms and legs against the door. Cho backs off and blasts into the door with four of his hollow-point bullets that explode open upon impact like deadly flower petals—particularly in soft tissue. The gunman moves on.

. . .

One floor above, biomechanics professor Kevin Granata rushes twenty-some horrified students into his office where they lock themselves inside. The developer of leading advancements in movement dynamics and cerebral palsy bolts down the stairs to investigate. The military veteran and father of three dies confronting the shooter.

In Room 211, Canadian-born Madame Jocelyne Couture-Nowak pauses in her Intermediate French class. "That's not what I think it is . . . is it?" she asks her students. Couture-Nowak opens the door, peeks into the hallway, and immediately slams the door.

Couture-Nowak blurts out, "Call 911." Seconds later she and most of her students lie in pools of bloods—most with multiple gunshot wounds. One is freshman Mary Read, also born in South Korea like her killer. Only one student, Clay Violand, stumbled out unscathed.

After blasting his way through the second floor of Norris, stone-silent Cho turns his weapon toward his own face, his own taut mouth. The world would now hear from this speechless loner.

The young man, who dubbed himself "Question Mark," left the stunned and the curious around the globe with one plaguing word . . . and a question mark of its own. *Why?*

Seung-Hui Cho rarely spoke. When he did, his voice jerked into deep guttural tones. He refused to say hello to anyone. Many thought he was mute. The senior English major didn't speak during his playwriting class last fall. He uttered no words when he sprayed more than 170 rounds of ammo into the flesh of his fellow Hokies. Heart-less Cho carried more than 200 additional rounds for maximum damage.

No words describe the horror that engulfed the sprawling Blacksburg campus in the aftermath of Cho's brutal rampage that killed twenty-seven students and five professors and ripped bullet holes into roughly twenty-five others. Few in the classroom killing fields escaped without injury.

Cho's failure to speak is not the only eerie thing about him that morning in West AJ and Norris. His hollow brown eyes appeared darkened with evil. He blankly stared at the people he gunned down, as if fixed on a distant ship at sea. Cho's cold, dead eyes still haunt his massacre survivors.

"I saw his eyes . . . that's probably the scariest thing. There was nothing there, just emptiness almost," sophomore Derek O'Dell recalls of Cho's rampage in the Elementary German class. "Like you can look in people's eyes and you can see life, their stories. But his—just emptiness."

With vacant, steely eyes, Seung-Hui Cho mercilessly ended innocent lives. If only another human could have grasped what the self-absorbed senior saw with his lifeless eyes. The violent shootings are not just a staggering loss for the Hokies. They are a sorrowful loss for all human-kind. Even God.

Yet even now, from behind the menacing shadows of Cho's gunfire melee, mourners at Virginia Tech, throughout America, and around the globe are lifting their eyes from their shock and grief to find the grace and peace that only their Creator can supply.

On this Blue Ridge Mountains campus blanketed by death, already gifts of strength and renewal rise from the devastation. For as the psalmist wrote centuries ago, "I will lift up my eyes to the mountains; from where shall my help come? My help comes from the Lord, who made heaven and earth" (Psalm 121:1–2, NASB).

Dear Love,   *8-16-06*

I'm at college! Yeah . . . funny, isn't it. The thing I pined for the most for a year suddenly feels empty.

I'm very excited to be here but I'm also very nervous (esp. due to band try-outs! I didn't do so hot on the auditions). I'm also TERRIFIED that this isn't where God wants me to be.

While showering I had a very calming thought. "Regardless what I should have done, or should be, this is where I am." Regret doesn't get me anywhere but putting it in God's (Your) hands takes care of EVERYTHING!

Desiring so much to be in marching band, shaking with fear that I won't make friends and missing my mother dearly (oh yes) all rips my emotions and heart to shreds. Though I don't know if this is where I'm supposed to be or if I'm going to fail at the things I set out to achieve, I do know that I will praise you, my Lord and God! I thank you for all you've done for me and I glorify your name for being God. You are merciful and forgiving, personal and caring, mighty and just, omniscient and all powerful and you are MY GOD. Take control of this existence and use me. Bring me friends that love you, truly love you, not just the religious. Take my worries and anxiety and take control (it feels like I'm missing something, Jesus, show me what it is). But it's late and tomorrow will be busy.

Love,

Lauren A. McCain

[From Lauren's journal]

CHAPTER TWO
"PLEASE CALL."

I just stopped answering my cell phone. After people knew I was all right, I wasn't up for talking, because I would just cry. I didn't really want to process losing people over and over and over again. So I stopped answering my phone.

—JULIE HARRISON, VIRGINIA TECH JUNIOR

In four Virginia Tech classrooms, cell phones ring . . . and ring . . . and ring—but no one answers them. RAZRs and other flip-ups tucked in jackets, crammed in bloody backpacks, or scattered amid overturned desks emit musical tones and steady vibrations. But their owners can no longer hear them.

That morning, twenty-year-old Lauren McCain didn't bring her cell phone to her German class in Norris 207. The night before, the International Studies freshman zipped off an e-mail to her parents, Dave and Sherry McCain, in Hampton, Virginia:

Subject: sup homes?

Date: Sun, 15 Apr 2007 19:10:07

Um, so while I was gone this weekend, I dropped my phone at a friend's house, outside, and left it, all night, and some of the next day, so it rained, and poured, and my phone DIDN'T die, but the battery ran out, and now I can't charge it, so, I'm phoneless, if you want to contact me, you'll have to write me an e-mail, or something, ok, love you bye

—lauren

I'm boycotting periods, and exclamation points

A short drive from the university, the Virginia Tech staff of Campus Crusade for Christ chat and sip coffee during their regular Monday morning team meeting. In his living room, CRU director Jeff Highfield is about to open his Bible and share devotional thoughts on pain and suffering. The phone rings alerting the CRU team of the initial shootings on campus.

The CRU leaders huddle around the television downstairs.

Jeff's wife, Lisa, driving home from an Ohio visit, receives a call on her cell phone from her sister. "Lisa, did you hear there were shootings on campus?" Confounded by the news of gunfire at peaceful Virginia

Tech, Lisa calls her husband and the staff team at her house.

Jeff confirms the report that two Virginia Tech students are dead. Lisa hangs up and thinks to call a friend in Blacksburg whose husband has a police scanner. "Lisa, it sounds like it's so much worse than just two. He's saying maybe twenty-nine." The mother of two-year-old and three-year-old daughters clenches the steering wheel. *Surely, this can't be right,* Lisa reasons.

Lisa calls her husband back with the sobering news of fatalities. Rushing south on West Virginia's I-77, she finds a radio station and listens to students on the Tech campus calling with in-the-moment testimonies of being locked down in academic buildings and watching police carry out bodies.

Trying to keep her eyes on the road, Lisa starts calling CRU students and disciples she knows. Many don't answer so, through tears, Lisa stammers on their voice mails, "I-I-I hope that you're okay. Please call me back. I want to make sure that you're okay. *Plea*se call me back."

"Please call me back." Hour after hour on that bleak springtime Monday, thousands of frantic parents, siblings, classmates, teachers, distant relatives, pastors, and long-lost friends express these same four pleading words: "Please call me back."

With the deluge of cell phone calls and text messages to and from the Blacksburg area that day, many people can't leave voice mails and some receive no service at all.

CRU student Dana Cox is in her organic chemistry lab when a classmate receives the all-campus e-mail about the shootings in West AJ. The lab group breaks for the day and Dana walks outside to call one of the students in her AJ freshman Bible study: Molly Donohue.

Dana asks Molly, who lives on fourth floor West AJ, if all the women in their CRU Bible study are okay. Molly cries hysterically.

"Wait. Molly, what's wrong?" Dana blurts out. "I know you're upset, but you gotta answer me."

"I-I-I can't, uh, explain right now," Molly replies between her gasping sobs. "Everyone in our study is okay."

The junior from Colonial Heights, Virginia, offers to meet with the traumatized freshman before a one o'clock class. Molly agrees to meet, but can't get out the words to express what she's witnessed that morning. In her daze she doesn't even know yet that her two friends, Emily Hilscher and Ryan Clark, were murdered—right next door.

It's now about 9:45 in the morning, and Dana is "freaking out about Molly" as she is walking onto the west side of Burruss, the university's administration building, which towers next to Norris. Suddenly the piercing *whooh-whooh-whur* of multiple police sirens wail out of nowhere. Two police cars slam to a halt in front of Dana. Officers wielding assault rifles bolt behind Burruss toward Norris.

Thinking the police presence is related to the incident in West AJ, Dana turns right and heads to nearby Williams Hall to check in with her Bible study coleader, Julie Harrison. In Williams, people congregate in the tight-spaced atrium—staying away from windows as instructed. Dana and Julie, a junior in psychology, see other students walking outside, so the two of them exit and drive home to the apartment complex where they live. The two sit mesmerized in front of Julie's television, watching live coverage of the increasing death tally of their fellow Hokies.

Across America, and other parts of the world, millions of concerned individuals gather around television sets, computer screens, and radios in homes, offices, coffee shops, anywhere they can catch a glimpse of the unfolding chaos in Blacksburg.

Whitney Apr 16 2007 10:44A

myspace.com comment to Lauren McCain

Please call me asap. I'm worried about you with all the news I heard this morning.

Montgomery Regional, the closest hospital to the Virginia Tech campus, is also the second smallest hospital in the entire Roanoke and New River valleys. The most seriously injured land in this nearby facility first; once stabilized, many transfer to larger trauma centers in Salem, Radford, and Roanoke.

Ambulance after ambulance roars up to the hospital's ER doors. A male with two gunshot wounds in a leg and one in an arm. A survivor with a gun blast to the chest. Two patients with bleeding abdomens.

Gowned and gloved surgeons scramble in operating rooms. Nurses comfort the less critically wounded. Patients' cell phones dance on and off feverishly. Injured students plead, "Have you called my mom?" For many, Mom has already called and is on her way.

Two hundred twenty-five miles away, along Virginia's southern coast, Mom Sherry McCain is helping her youngest children, Christian, ten, and Abby, seven, with their homeschool assignments. Dave McCain, a chief petty officer with the Navy, is at work.

The phone rings, interrupting Sherry's efforts with her son and daughter. A niece is calling to find out if Sherry has heard about the dormitory shootings at Lauren's campus. Not much of a worrier, Sherry figures Lauren must be safe because her reliably responsible daughter would call immediately if she were affected by the dormitory incident.

About fifteen minutes later, at 10:45, a friend calls and informs Sherry about other shootings in Norris Hall. "Lauren is not an engineering student, I can't imagine her having any classes in that hall," Sherry reassures her friend. "She's probably just fine."

When Dave hears about the mayhem at Lauren's school, he calls Sherry to check about their oldest daughter, then drives home about 11:30. Before long, family and friends, including friends from the McCains' church, Restoration Church—Phoebus Baptist, come over to wait and pray. A friend takes the kids to a talent show practice.

Apr 16 2007 1:24P

myspace.com comment to Lauren McCain

Call your parents asap

Dave calls Lauren's East AJ roommate to see if she has heard from Lauren, but can't reach Jessica. When he finally speaks to Jessica at 4:30 P.M., she tells him she last saw Lauren at around 9:00 when she was heading to class. Sherry calls Jessica again about an hour later.

"Lauren didn't have any classes in Norris Hall . . . did she?" Sherry asks.

"Yes. She did," Jessica replies. "I saw Lauren just before she was going to 207 for her German class."

The news punches deeply. Immediately Dave and Sherry arrange for Christian and Abby to stay with friends, toss a few things in an overnight bag, and drive west toward Blacksburg.

On the drive, at first both husband and wife say little. At one point, Dave breaks the silence. "I know that the worst case for us would be the best case for Lauren." Sherry reads several Scripture passages aloud. Together they pray, offering their beloved Lauren into God's hands.

"We were praying for a miracle. Knowing Lauren, she would have called us immediately, gotten online, let somebody know she was fine," Sherry explains. "She would have been ministering to other students. We prayed over and over that somehow God would be glorified through this horrible situation. We kept praying for a miracle."

Thoughts come to each of their minds as they make their difficult journey westward: *Our blue-eyed daughter is probably helping others at the scene. Toned, physically, from playing intramural soccer and flag football, maybe our high-energy Lauren helped accost the shooter. Maybe she is slightly injured in a hospital. Maybe Lauren escaped the campus in her 1999 Saturn SL listening to CDs of Christian artists*

TobyMac or Super Chicks. (Lauren likes her "radical" Christian music, forget country and western.) Or maybe . . . just maybe, God wants Lauren more in her heavenly home than her earthly one.

Sherry's sister, Tracie, calls while Dave and Sherry race to the Hokie campus.

"Lauren wasn't in German class, was she?" Tracie inquires. "Oh, Sherry, I think only four people got out alive from that classroom."

Almost everyone who knows Lauren prays for a miracle. They e-mail her and try her cell phone. If relatives and friends do get through via the phone lines, they hear Lauren's offbeat voice mail:

Ultimate ruler of the universe.

Prayers and petitions: press one.

Acceptable sacrifices: press two.

Unacceptable sacrifices: press pound.

Adoration and praise, please hold for the first customer-
*   service representative.*

Current wait time: Eternity.

Thank you for your time.

(Dave McCain's voice) **Get off the phone and clean**
*   **your room!** (Lauren's giggle)*

Monday afternoon at the Highfields', the Campus Crusade staff team works on an action plan. Jeff and Lisa, Dave and Susan Broadwell, Blair and Sarah Pippin, Mike Stevenson (his wife, Laura, is at home with their three little ones), and Paul and Cynthia Thomas, all start calling the CRU students directly under their leadership. Each student is asked to check in with his or her own Bible study students. With some five hundred student regulars involved in the Virginia Tech ministry, it takes a while to get a full accounting of everyone's safety. Blair Pippin reaches one of the guys in his Bible study, junior computer engineering student Ruiqi (*RICH-ie*) Zhang. Ruiqi recounts that fateful day:

I call my girlfriend at James Madison University before her 8:00 class. I just want to say "hi" before getting ready for my 9:05 computer-science class in Norris Hall.

I walk from my dorm across the Drillfield to Norris. I walk fast and arrive at Room 205 earlier than usual. About 9:40 or so, I hear loud banging and a girl scream. I first think it's construction going on and the girl is startled by it.

Everyone in class hears the sounds, but we think it's some worker in the building next door banging on the wall with a hammer. The sounds boom again, so our teaching assistant, who is lecturing for the day, looks into the hallway with a student who is close to the door.

They immediately shut the door and our TA yells, "Get down." A graduate student runs up to the door and steels himself against it. The rest of us drop to the floor. Some kids call 911 on their cell phones.

After a bit we gain our composure and some guys push a coffee table and desk against the door. I'm lying down about five feet from the door. I am so scared—a kind of fear-for-my-life scared. I pray over and over again, *God, keep us safe. Watch over us.*

We hear gunshots and the shots get muffled as the shooter goes into rooms. The gunfire is clearer when he is in the hallway. It sounds like he is moving up and down the hall. He soon tries our door. He puts some force into slamming against our door.

He shoots twice into the door. One bullet strikes the podium. The other hits a window. I am just praying and praying that the gunman will not get through our door.

All ten students and our TA in the room stay real quiet. The shooter backs away from the door and reloads his gun. I hear the clicking of the magazine coming out and then he puts in another one.

We all fear he will come at us again, but he leaves. Some girls are crying. Two students talk on cell phones with the police dispatcher. We stay on the floor. After 10:00, maybe 10:15, the police yell outside our door to "open up."

Down the hallway, I can hear other police officers yelling, "Get your hands up, get down" and "Men down! We need a medic in here." I realize the situation is pretty serious.

Running down the hallway to get out of the building, I see a giant pool of blood on the floor with lines leading away from it like someone dragged a body along. The class and I stay locked down in another engineering building, talking to each other as we wait. About noon the state police and ATF people take statements from all of us who are witnesses in Norris.

Now I definitely feel a kinship with my classmates and teaching assistant—we survived and kept the shooter out of our room. We realize we are really blessed because nobody in the room got hurt. I don't know why Cho did what he did. I just know that God was watching over us that day.

Through all this, I'm asking myself, *What kind of life am I living? Does my life honor God?* I realize that I need to have a strong relationship with God and I want to be more involved with CRU. I know now that I could die any day. A couple of Christian friends from the class and I believe that God kept us alive for a reason. We just have to find that reason.

The Bible basically says live for today, tomorrow is not guaranteed. That's hit me pretty hard since the shootings. You don't know when you're going to die, so you need to trust that God is in charge of everything and everything will be all right.

Wanting to see if everything is all right with their Bible-study women, Dana Cox and Julie Harrison meet up with the CRU staff at the Highfields' Monday afternoon. Word is spreading among the students that Molly lives close to the two slain students in West AJ. Dana and Julie ask for their CRU leaders to pray for Molly, whom they can't reach via cell phone.

Initial reports Monday reveal that two Campus Crusade students die in Norris. One, Jarrett Lane, in Professor Loganathan's hydrology class, is less than four weeks from graduating. The other, nineteen-year-old freshman Mary Read, is undecided about a major but not undecided about following Jesus.

One student connected with CRU throughout the 2005–2006 school year witnesses his entire classroom killed or injured. He walks out without a wound. At least one CRU student is missing—Lauren McCain.

Monday at 7 P.M., several of the Virginia Tech Christian ministries, as well as community members, gather at the Baptist Collegiate Ministries (BCM) building right on the east edge of campus for a time of prayer and support. Two questions bounce around the CRU group: Have you *heard* from Lauren McCain? Have you *seen* Lauren McCain? Dana and Julie gather their Bible study on the well-dated green couches on the top floor of the BCM building. Freshmen Janelle Frasier and Sarah Olmstead help console a visibly shaken Molly. No one is quite sure what Molly encountered.

I am in chem lab and my roommate texts me, *The police want to talk to you.* I get excused from lab and start to run back to my dorm, but I am crying so hard because I fear that Emily, Heather, and Ryan are dead. I am crying so much I can't run. People walking to class look at me like I'm a crazy person. I am literally convulsing as I run crying.

I finally have to just speed walk across the Drillfield. It's snowing and I'm freezing. I approach the front entrance to my dorm and see all these ambulances and police cars. Immediately several cops approach me and ask, "Are you Molly Donohue?"

They pull me inside and take me into the back room where a male and female Virginia Tech police officer question me. I describe the man blocking the door in Emily and Heather's room as if he were an intruder. I didn't see his face. I am in such shock and it doesn't occur to me who this guy could be.

Later a bunch of friends, mainly from CRU, and I gather in the third floor West AJ lounge. Everyone sits there in shock. We pray and then talk, and then pray some more. Down the hall we hear people watching the TV coverage on the shootings yell, "It's up to ten. Now it's up to twenty." No one is allowed to leave the dorms, so we just pray together. We constantly hear sirens. No one's cell phones are working, and everyone's family is trying to call. It just feels like extreme chaos.

Since no one has heard from Lauren, Dana and Julie's study group, along with Lauren's spiritual mentor, Chum Hoang, go look for Lauren themselves. Not wanting to burden Molly with more upsetting news, they leave Molly at the meeting.

Together the five young women walk the ten minutes

to Lauren's East AJ dorm room. In some ways they are like the downhearted women headed to Jesus' tomb. They discover that Lauren is the only one on her dorm floor unaccounted for.

Walking away from Lauren's dorm, the coeds break out in tears. Dana, the one typically cool in panic situations, tries to encourage her friends with, "Lauren is a real independent gal, and she could have just left Norris. We don't even know she was even in the building." The attempts at morale boosting fall short on her grieving friends' ears. Inside all of their hurting hearts, they fear the worst.

James Apr 16 2007 7:44P

myspace.com comment to Lauren McCain

Hey lil' Cuz. Give us a call and let us no that you are all right. We are worried about you.

At the BCM prayer time, the CRU director Jeff Highfield shares a few words with the troubled CRU students. "If you haven't talked to anybody, do that. Talk about what you're feeling. Talk about your experience," Jeff explains, looking around the group, ashen-faced with sadness and sorrow. "You need to let yourself go emotionally *up to my room and as I pass the hall doors Ashley (a really nice girl that I'd met earlier in the day) went running past, soaking wet, saying she'd left the fan on and the windows open. I follow (she's started talking to me so it would be rude to ignore) and we walk into her room. Offering to shut her window (she's wet and the bed's in the way) I do it for her. Then she tells me she didn't get to have supper so I invite her to go with me!*

Even if we don't become bosom buddies I do think God is providing for me even in the small things.

Thank You!

♥ *Lauren*

(someday, well . . . early next morning)

Is anyone among you suffering? Let him pray . . . and the Lord will raise him up.

James 5:13–15

[From Lauren's journal]

wherever it is. Just do that. The staff and I care about you. We're here if you want to talk. We're here to pray with you. We all need each other now—perhaps more than ever."

After the meeting, Julie, Molly, Janelle, and Sarah all hang out at Dana's apartment. No one wants to leave Molly alone. One minute she sobs uncontrollably. The next she stares blankly.

Dana gives the worn-out Molly a sleep aid and they all crash in the living room on Dana's blue futon and a mattress on the floor watching a lighthearted movie, *The Wedding Date.* When Molly tries to fall asleep she sees flashbacks of the bloody shoeprints outside her room . . . and hears Emily's horrible scream.

Sometime after midnight, Julie heads to her own adjacent apartment, but at 2:30 A.M. sends a text message to Dana.

You up?

Yes, Dana shoots back.

I can't sleep. I'm coming over.

The two juniors lie awake in Dana's room softly talking until 4:00 A.M. about Monday's excruciating events and their three Bible-study gals all curled up together on the futon in the living room. Molly in the middle.

Whitney Apr 17 2007 11:56A

myspace.com comment to Lauren McCain

Oh Lauren please call someone. We are so worried about you. We miss you so much.

8-18-06

Oh my! You are sooooo wonderful! I'll have to write about my band experience later but the coolest thing just happened!

I just went through the most depressing 30 minutes of my life! I was bawling before God because I'm all alone at this scary college place not knowing anyone, not being the best social person and all in all just miserable.

I opened my Bible and read in Isaiah that God tends His vineyard and no one can hurt it. The vineyard being Israel and no one can hurt them, but I applied it to me. I begged God for someone to come and be with me, a sister in Christ! Well as I read it went to another passage about God and His loving kindness, how merciful He is and I realized this is temporary! But God, He's forever.

After I cried and bawled some I decided to go for a ⟨ Right then it started POURING, so I walked downstai stare somewhat forlornly into the rain. (By now God h stored my peace but I was still a tad bit lonesome.)

Since there was nothing I could do outside I wall

CHAPTER THREE
LIGHTS IN THE DARKNESS

This guy drew our blood, but he
will not draw our spirit.

—STEVE SCHNEITER, VIRGINIA TECH GRADUATE STUDENT

Monday night plenty of people in the Blacksburg area toss and turn in their beds. Not just Molly Donohue and her Bible-study girls. Some locals dream of creepy black-cloaked demons battling angels of light. Some experience nightmares over their experiences at the hand of Cho. Others wrestle with being called in by police to help identify the gunman's body.

Thinking the killer might be a mechanical engineering student, police had called the school's mechanical engineering professors to come to the station to help identify a possible shooter. One professor is Andrew Duggleby, who was minutes away from teaching a 10:10 class that morning on Norris's second floor. Professor Duggleby views a crime-scene photograph of the killer still lying in his own blood. But the engineering instructor isn't sure he's ever seen the student before.

After looking at the full-color photo of the lifeless Cho, the professor goes home and can't bear to see the killer's face flashed constantly on the television screen. The Christian professor stumbles for words when he eventually tells his wife about examining Cho's photographed face up close.

"You see dead bodies on television and you see gunshot wounds on television, but it's not real. This photo was real. Even his eyelids were a different color," Duggleby eventually confides in his wife.

The reality that this student had slaughtered so many fellow Hokies rattles the composure of most individuals left to sort through the messy crime-scene evidence and fuzzy details of the killer's puzzling life. Sobered by the combat-zone remnants in Norris Hall, one police officer declares, "It feels like the devil has been released here today."

In the hours after the last gunshot echoed in Norris 211, even people with a deep trust in God's abiding presence wrestle with the possibility and fear that the campus murderer might have an accomplice who could still attack out of nowhere.

"Monday night I only slept a half hour because I am just so overwhelmed with the aftermath of everything," CRU member Lisa Highfield explains. "I was just full of fear because there was no confirmation that only one shooter was involved. At times I worried that another gunman could be in my own backyard."

Another fear grips the Asians students in Blacksburg, particularly those of Korean descent: fear of retaliation because the shooter was South Korean. With some two thousand international students who study and conduct graduate research at the Virginia Polytechnic Institute and State University, the vast majority are from India and China.

Once news breaks that the killer is Korean-born, most Asians living on or around the Virginia Tech campus rush to their dorm rooms, apartments, and houses. They lock their doors and refuse to venture outside for a day or two.

Erin Carter, a Virginia Tech osteopathy medical student, describes a "spirit of fear" that seems to suffocate Blacksburg and neighboring communities in the wake of the massacre. "All night long I was fighting in my sleep with spiritual warfare," Erin says. "I wasn't particularly afraid of anything. I could just feel fear all around me."

When the sun pokes its rosy glow across the eastern

horizon at 6:44 A.M. on Tuesday, April 17, fear and anxiety still hover in the minds and hearts of thousands directly affected by the mass murder in their midst.

Virginia Tech CRU staff member Cynthia Thomas writes in an April 17 Campus Crusade blog:

Strangely, I had a dream the night before the shootings about a gunman mowing down people at random. I actually have disturbing dreams like that often, so I forgot about it until the middle of the day. Yesterday I felt numb and in shock. Today I am overwhelmed with sadness and stress.

I found out first thing this morning that one of the students in our movement was confirmed dead. What a terrible moment. Our team is very close and very much a family, so it was great for us all to be together and process a little. We cried, prayed. I wish we could have done that for longer. Moving into "work mode" was excruciating for me. I keep thinking, *How can I minister and love and care for these students, when I need those things myself?*

Cynthia hears about one shooting survivor, junior Clay Violand, who played bass guitar in the CRU band his freshman year. Cynthia types in her blog:

I was sickened to think about what he endured and will continue to remember for the rest of his life.

Clay later shares his near-death experience:

Our French class is about halfway over, when we hear a bunch of loud noises down the hallway that don't stop. Our teacher tenses up and asks, "That's not what I think it is . . . is it?"

I immediately start to panic. I shout at Madame Couture-Nowak, "Put that desk in front of the door. Right now!"

She slides the desk to the door and yells, "Call 911!" Colin Goddard, on my right, jumps up and makes the call. He's talking on his cell when the door pops open. I see this gun—then this young-looking Asian guy. He's wearing some kind of utility belt stuffed with a ton of ammunition. I only catch a glimpse of him.

I dive under my desk. I prepare to die right there. Gunfire bangs around the room. It's as if the shooter is slowly, one by one, picking off my classmates. Every time I hear a shot, I close my eyes tighter, and think, *The next one is for me.*

Sometimes after a shot, I hear a quick moan or a

slow one. Sometimes a grunt. I hear one of the girls trying to yell out. I am totally numb. I play like I'm dead. The person on my right is hit, then on my left. I feel nothing. I just lie there as lifeless as possible.

I pray in my head that God will put an invisible blanket of protection around me. Finally the shooting stops. I stay with my face pressed to the floor, trying to fake that I'm not breathing. I hold my breath . . . and wait.

The room is silent except for some haunting moans. I hear some crying. Someone mutters, "It's okay. It's going to be okay. They will be here soon." I prop my head up a bit and mutter, "Play dead. If he thinks you're dead, he won't kill you."

But seconds later, the gunman returns. I stay motionless against the floor. The shooter unloads another round into everyone again—it has to be the same people. He fires way more bullets than the number of us in the room. He reloads about three times. The guys shoots my classmates over and over.

I brace for the next bullet to hit me. My thoughts stray. *What will a bullet wound feel like? I hope it doesn't hurt. Will I die slow or fast?* Yet, somehow the shooter skips over me . . . several times. I keep thinking about my parents and how they'll have to go on without me. This terrifies me more.

A girl lying in front of me makes eye contact. I don't know her name. From time to time our eyes meet. She's brave and doesn't cry. We stare at each other under the desks. I think she's hit in the back. Every bullet misses me. I don't get it.

Eventually the shooting stops. I hear the police barge into the hallway doors. I hear them yell, "Get down! Get down!" The cops get in our room and tell us to get up and walk out if we can. Just the girl next to me and I stand and put our hands up. We are the only two in our class to walk out. She has a gunshot wound, but I am so proud of her for staying calm. If I died, she would have been the last person I made eye contact with on Earth.

. . .

While Clay remains motionless on the classroom floor, which is now splattered and smeared with blood, his wounded classmate Colin Goddard eyes the killer's shoes—just inches away. Seung-Hui Cho stands right next to Colin and fires a bullet into Colin's shoulder and buttocks to accompany his leg wound.

Cho moves to the front of the classroom. *Bang. Bang.* Almost immediately after those final two shots, police storm the room yelling, "Shooter down! Black tag!" America's worst mass execution by gunfire is now over.

Six weeks after the shootings on campus, Clay, a twenty-year-old international studies major, reflects about his horrifying experience in Norris 211. "I am recovering well. I just occupy myself with work and friends. Sometimes I break down, but most of the time things are normal.

"I don't know how this has affected me spiritually. I don't know if I was spared. It's difficult for me to see it that way. I think it's too soon. Perhaps I just got lucky. I really don't know. But I do feel like seeking out God now."

One corollary of the campus murders is that many people have the desire to seek God. Some through prayer, often punctuated with anger and tears. Others through the comfort of clergy and trained trauma counselors. Anxious family members congregate inside The Inn at Virginia Tech and Skelton Conference Center, with its upscale but casual accommodations, located just on the edge of campus along Prices Fork Road.

When the wait for confirmation of a son's or daughter's death weighs too heavily, some loved ones escape to the nearby Duck Pond, appropriately lined with weeping willows. Monday's shock and numbness is thawing trickle by trickle, like a slow dripping faucet. *Plop. Plunk. Plop. Plunk.*

Time nudges forward, but ever too painfully for the family and friends of twenty-seven murdered collegians and five murdered professors.

Dave and Sherry McCain, bolstered by their pastor and close friends, wait for their own meeting with the coroner. One lone father at the Inn shuffles and paces, anticipating his worst nightmare coming true. Dave and Sherry extend words of comfort and concern to the man, then give him a compassionate embrace. Minutes later this father learns his eighteen-year-old didn't survive.

For now, this private group of the grieving is secluded from the hordes of journalists and camera crews that are descending on the typically serene campus—like famished ants at a summer picnic.

"This is not how we live in southwest Virginia, you don't see Katie Couric walking down the street or Matt Lauer eating at the Outback," says local resident Sandra Jackson. "This is just not our life. Blacksburg is an ordinary place to live."

Local and major national news networks, and many stations from abroad, invade Blacksburg: NBC, ABC, CBS, CNN, FOX, Larry, Brian, Katie, Rush, Greta, Stone, Nancy, the *Washington Post*, the *New York Times*, *Newsweek*,

Time, People. Reporters from Spain, Norway, France, and Japan join the media whirl of microphones and cameras. Satellite dishes beam accounts of the gruesome murders to the curious and the heartbroken around the globe. Leaving Virginia Tech's family little privacy to begin their mourning.

National media celebrities are not the only visitors in town. Virginia Governor Tim Kaine and President George W. Bush arrive Tuesday to speak to ten thousand at the 2:00 P.M. Memorial Convocation in Cassell Coliseum. An overflow crowd of twenty thousand gathers in nearby Lane Stadium to watch a big-screen simulcast, while thousands of Blacksburg residents stay home to watch on television. A solemn nation joins them.

For Dana Cox and Julie Harrison and a handful of other Campus Crusade students sitting in the coliseum audience together, the convocation soon blurs with heavy tears. Somewhere amid university officials' comments and leaders' prayers. Somewhere amid Nikki Giovanni exclaiming, "We are the Hokies. We will prevail," and poignant speeches by the governor and President Bush, a fresh wave of grief crashes over these CRU students.

Dana's friend Tom gets a text message from his friend Andy, who received a text message from the boyfriend of Lauren's roommate. Tom leans forward and whispers into

Dana's ear. "I don't know how to tell you this. But, Lauren didn't make it."

Moments earlier at the Inn, Dave and Sherry McCain are the last of the Virginia Tech parents to learn about their child, who had been gunned down by a fellow student some thirty hours earlier.

"We were told the medical examiner was coming to talk to us. It was like a doctor coming out after surgery," says Dave. "By then, we needed somebody to tell us the facts, to be out of gray, into the black and the white."

The medical examiner delivers the news they have been dreading and hands them a photograph so they can identify their daughter.

"We saw the picture of Lauren's face, and she looked peaceful, like she was sleeping," Sherry recalls.

The coroner reassured Dave and Sherry that Lauren died instantly from a bullet to her head and one nick to her neck. Police believe Cho shot German professor Jamie Bishop first, then aimed next at Lauren sitting in the front row, closest to the door.

In remembering the excruciating wait to hear about Lauren, Julie Harrison says, "It was horrible being in limbo. But it was worse and a devastating realization to learn that Lauren was gone."

Gone is the daughter who would call her father at work and blurt out, "Dad, I have ten minutes. Tell me about Middle East politics." Gone is the friend who praised God so joyfully in prayer that others longed to be in her group when it was time to pray.

Gone is Lauren Ashley McCain, December 20, 1986, to April 16, 2007. Gone but not forgotten.

Two other CRU students, senior Jarrett Lane and freshman Mary Read, are gone, too. Jarrett, the high-school sports standout and valedictorian from tiny Narrows, Virginia, just some twenty miles from Virginia Tech. Mary, a nineteen-year-old with an infectious smile, who proudly played clarinet for her alma mater in the northern Virginia suburb of Annandale.

In times like this, we can find comfort in the grace and guidance of a loving God. As the Scriptures tell us, "Don't be overcome by evil, but overcome evil with good." . . . It's impossible to make sense of such violence and suffering. Those whose lives were taken did nothing to deserve their fate. They were simply in the wrong place at the wrong time. Now they're gone— and they leave behind grieving families, and grieving classmates, and a grieving nation.

—PRESIDENT GEORGE W. BUSH

· · ·

As darkness closes in Tuesday upon Blacksburg, some thirty thousand mourners spread out on the grassy Drill-field nestled between the sites of the multiple shootings. The West AJ dormitory is to the south, Norris Hall to the north.

The dead are honored with sobs, hugs, moments of silence, and the singing of "The Star Spangled Banner" and "Amazing Grace." Through the darkest moments in the history of this university, the bereaved lift flickering candles upward. Through some of the darkest moments ever lived in world history, many also lift their eyes toward heaven.

You will always remember the friends and teachers who were lost yesterday, and the time you shared with them, and the lives they hoped to lead.

—PRESIDENT GEORGE W. BUSH

Apr 17 2007 11:23P
myspace.com comment to Lauren McCain
Lauren I love you so much. I dont want to say goodbye so

Ill just say that Ill see you later in our Lords kingdom where we will have plenty of time to catch up. You were so beautiful when i saw you this easter and I will always remember you that way. love always..... your cousin....
James

I'm really struggling, it's like I get depressed and I can't take it to Him; I don't want to; I don't know but I'm afraid He'll let me down, that I'll just be some loser, I don't know.

But He talked to me on the way back from recitation and just being with Him puts everything into perspective. So, when I had another bout (I was going to say attack—but that gave me tingles) I picked up His word (smart—I know) and my "Life song" as I termed it (long ago, mind you) was there. Psalm 37 "Trust in the Lord and do good. Dwell in the land and FEED on His faithfulness."

I'm in this "land" (and I really wouldn't trade it for anything else) but it isn't happy—well—it isn't peaceful. But I will dwell here and I will feed on His faithfulness.

Rest in the Lord; I wait patiently for Him. Delight myself in the Lord, and He'll give me the desires of my Heart!

If that's actually giving my heart what it should desire, or giving it what it desires now, I don't know. But either way, it's good!

When I was talking to him I mentioned the fact that I was "stuck" in this limbo, that I wasn't growing in Him. He gently brought to mind that; 1—He's always growing me, and 2—growing pains—lol—when in the valley, you can't not grow. I was trying to describe the thing that I thought was causing my distress and I remember thinking that when I got to college I would be used by Him! I would be glorifying Him with the church here—perhaps I should stop whining, lean on Him, and just live.

OK, enough moping, I've got homework and then, well, I'm going out. ☺ *(to cru—lol—)*

♥ *Lauren*

[From Lauren's journal]

CHAPTER FOUR
THE LOVE OF MY LIFE

Lauren was outspoken about her love for
Christ; more so than any other person
I had ever met on a college campus.
She called him the love of her life.

—ALLIE BURGIN, VIRGINIA TECH SOPHOMORE

In southwest Virginia on the morning of April 16, God's faithful were injured and murdered along with those yet to walk with him. Some reports figure that approximately ten of the thirty-two fallen were known followers of Jesus.

The television and magazine updates portray these Christians among rows of tiny photos with brief biography blurbs. Brian Bluhm, a huge Hokie fan. Rachael Hill, an accomplished pianist. Erin Peterson, a talented basketball player. These clipped descriptions miss the rich, soulful character of all of the incredible young believers.

While loner Cho festered over "Christian Criminals" who supposedly mistreated and humiliated him, these collegiate Christ-followers lived lives quite the opposite. The three lost CRU students, Mary Read, Jarrett Lane, and Lauren McCain, are among these brave hearts with an overflowing faith. Both Mary and Lauren were scheduled to receive an e-mail on the afternoon of April 16, congratulating them on being accepted as CRU Bible-study leaders starting in the fall. Both families wept when they later heard this news.

When Mary's family found a small red notebook among Mary's dorm room belongings, they flipped through the three years of journal entries. A few notations seemed to jump off the pages and bring Mary's lovable smile to life once again.

Never stop smiling, because you'll never know who is falling in love with it.

Two months before Cho pulled the trigger that ended Mary's life, the vivacious nineteen-year-old wrote prophetic words inspired by Paul Boese in her red notebook.

When a deep injury is done to us, we never recover until we forgive . . . forgiveness does not change the past, but it does enlarge the future.

Reeling from the "deep injury" inflicted on them all, relatives and friends paid their final tribute to the Virginia Tech freshman at St. Mary of Sorrows Catholic Church in Fairfax Station, Virginia. The name of the family's church so poignantly describes the deep sadness over the loss of God's ever-smiling child.

> Je t'adore mon amie. *Your smile will have my heart forever.*
>
> —HANDWRITTEN MESSAGE ON MARY'S
> WHITE CASKET

. . .

A month to the date of the killings, May 16, just-graduated Virginia Tech senior Brandon Overby sits in the Starbucks a few blocks west of campus. Brandon sips his White Chocolate Caffé Mocha, swirling it around so the sweetness doesn't all settle to the bottom of the mug. Brandon's blue-eyed gaze drifts out the window toward the university, the place where he lost his buddy Jarrett Lane.

"Jarrett loved the Lord. He wasn't as overt as some people in their faith, but he had a real deep passion for God. The legacy Jarrett has left me is to be much more intentional with my friendships. He did this right,"

Brandon says, with a smile edging its way onto his boyish face.

"The shootings have reminded me that our lives are but a vapor. We don't know how much time we have on this earth and we need to make the most out of our lives today. Part of that is just loving people to the point where they start noticing that something is different about your life."

The twenty-three-year-old pauses. He swallows hard. "Losing Jarrett and others has made me realize that there is more to life and more to my faith than just the day-to-day. What's more important are the relationships you develop with people, the love that you give to people to point them toward Christ.

"I may not understand what God chooses to do with all of his clay pots. But if he takes some of them home, God be praised. If he chooses to keep some people alive and take others away, then that's up to him. I know that God has a purpose and he is in control. He has better plans for us than we can ever know."

. . .

As with Jarrett's and Mary's deaths, the sudden loss of Lauren smacks against the hearts of those who knew her. Yet a sweet beginning to Lauren's legacy gently ripples across the

Blacksburg campus and beyond, eventually reaching untold millions who read her compelling MySpace words:

> The purpose and love of my life is Jesus Christ. I don't have to argue religion, philosophy, or historical evidence because I KNOW Him. He is just as real, if not more so, as my "earthly" father.

Finding God to be real and then wholeheartedly living out this conviction, Lauren the warm conversationalist influenced people when she wasn't even trying. Allie Burgin is one of these people. The Virginia Tech hospitality-and-tourism-management sophomore writes of how Lauren brushed against her heart.

> On Tuesday afternoon, as the names and pictures of the victims began to appear more frequently, I felt sick. I heard on the news that one of the classrooms the shooter had entered was a German classroom.
>
> At that very moment I became worried. I knew that one of the girls that I sat next to in my economics class took a lot of German classes. She always crammed for her German tests as the econ professors rambled about supply and demand or GDP. She and I didn't have a lot in common, besides our lack of economic

knowledge, so we never exchanged phone numbers or even e-mail addresses.

I realized I didn't even know her last name, just her first name—Lauren. But I had sat beside her through two semesters of economics. I just prayed she was okay. I had no way of getting in contact with her. . . . As my father scrolled through an online list of victims Tuesday evening, I saw Lauren's picture. Monday's tragedy up until that very point in time affected me greatly, but when I saw Lauren's picture on the computer screen, Monday became very personal.

Putting a familiar face among all the lost lives in this hateful crime left me empty. I hated that I only knew Lauren as the girl that took German and sat beside me in economics class. I hated that I hadn't made more of an effort to befriend her beyond the classroom. When I saw Lauren's picture among the victims my heart broke as I finally learned her last name.

I haven't forgotten one thing I learned about Lauren in those econ classes. Lauren was outspoken about her love for Christ; more so than any other person I had ever met on a college campus. She called him the love of her life. I do not think her smile will ever leave my mind.

Lauren Ashley McCain will never leave the minds of those close family and friends who mourn her short but well-lived life. Her death elicits their tears, their remembrances, their longings for heaven, too. When the darkness of sorrow closes in, the words of the long-suffering Job—who, in one day, lost all of his ten children—assures Lauren's loved ones that God gives and takes away, but he can always be trusted.

> . . . *"Naked I came from my mother's womb, and naked I will depart. The Lord gave and the Lord has taken away; may the name of the Lord be praised."*
> —JOB 1:21 (NIV)

The heartbeat of Lauren was to lift her eyes and her praise to her Creator. One high-school youth group friend says, "When we watched Lauren praise God, it was like she was reaching up and touching God's face, like she was trying to escape her body."

Dave and Sherry find restful comfort in knowing that their joyful daughter has escaped her earthly body to praise God in person. "Lauren was so passionate for Christ in her praise, her worship, and her prayer," Sherry says. "It's very easy for us to see her praising God because on Earth her worship was so wholehearted."

Lauren rarely put ho-hum effort into anything. Even when the spunky brunette prepared for college, she decided to dye her hair completely pink.

"People would say, 'How can you let your daughter do that?' I said, 'Why not? She loves the Lord, she's not rebellious. If this is how she wants to express something fun, I want to be part of it,'" Sherry explains. "I was glad Lauren was being expressive in standing out. The pink was better than a tattoo, which she also wanted. But I never felt comfortable with the tattoo idea, so Lauren honored my wishes."

Lauren's honor and respect for her parents was obvious to her newfound family of Hokies. Older brother Joel graduated from Virginia Tech and paved a path with Campus Crusade for Lauren to follow. Lauren, like Joel, enjoyed befriending international students, and she, too, signed up to be a language partner through Bridges, the ministry's outreach to internationals studying at the university.

Bridges director at Virginia Tech Blair Pippin sat in a training session Lauren led for language partner leaders the Thursday night before her death. "One word describes Lauren—passionate," Blair says. "She prayed with joy and she prayed with passion. I remember Lauren that night telling God, 'God, you're just so awesome.'"

At freshman orientation, when asked what mark she

wanted to leave upon her campus and the world, Lauren exclaimed, "I want everyone to know I love Jesus!" Lauren's desire to reflect Jesus to everyone flourishes well beyond her final moments taking notes in her German class. Already, because of the deaths of Lauren and her Christian friends, dozens of people are turning to the Savior these valiant ones adored.

Fellow believers are mobilizing around those deeply affected by the tragedy and loss. Immediately after the violence in Norris Hall, a group of Christians rallied around a distressed survivor who had endured the gunfire torture. This young man escaped a shot in the head from Cho—twice.

Cho, just feet away from the terrified student, aims, fires . . . and misses. Cho walks off as his attempted target starts shaking hysterically. When Cho returns to the classroom, he fires again at the jittery student still standing where Cho left him. Again, the bullet misses.

The traumatized suvivor is not sure about a faith in God, but day by day, he's seeing glimpses of Jesus' compassion and tenderness in his friends.

· · ·

Born in central Oklahoma, Lauren was a tribal member of the Choctaw nation and throughout her childhood moved with her family to several Navy coastal assignments. The McCains moved to Virginia's coast in 2001, where Lauren played soccer throughout high school. Her fall semester at Virginia Tech, Lauren long balled and chip shot her way into intramural soccer.

But the CRU women's Powder Puff football team is where everyone saw another side to the gentle, compassionate Lauren. In some ways, Powder Puff for Lauren was actually *Power* Puff.

Her father is quick to chuckle about watching his feisty daughter on the gridiron. "After she'd knock you down," Dave says, "she'd help you up and apologize."

Lauren would run, block, and tackle with exuberant might . . . all in Jesus' love, of course.

High-school friend Amy Yates remembers "wrestling" in the church parking lot back in Hampton, Virginia. "We always scuffled. I'd come up to her, bump into her. If I'd go after her, I always ended up on the ground," Amy concedes. "Lauren had this funny way of scooping my legs out from under me, with her hands under my back. In two seconds, she could lay me on the ground."

Lauren's rough-and-tumble energy was balanced by her girlish tenderness. "Both of us were really touch oriented. Any time Lauren was nervous, we'd just hold hands," Amy explains with fondness. "She'd pinch my hands to death watching scary movies or when we just needed to comfort each other."

After their 2007 spring-break ski trip, an exhausted Lauren laid her head in Amy's lap and fell asleep with Amy massaging her head. "That was kind of our love language," Amy says, recalling sweet memories of her full-of-life confidant.

Lauren's closest friend at Virginia Tech, Chum Hoang, took Lauren's death especially hard. Campus Crusade junior Chum discipled Lauren and coached her in Bridges. On weekends, the two were virtually inseparable. Fridays after classes the twosome would zip to the grocery store, then head to Chum's quaint brick rental house to whip together mounds of spaghetti, pancakes, or chili for a dinner discussion with up to forty Virginia Tech internationals.

Lauren would sleep over at Chum's and on Saturday mornings help her spiritual mentor host thirty students in a Campus Crusade Bible study. Neighbors continually saw hordes of people from other lands come and go behind Chum's white picket fence. To take a break from all the people, Lauren and Chum would play on the park swings off of Giles Road, sometimes swinging high like giggly grade-schoolers, sometimes sitting in silence just letting the breeze kiss their cheeks.

"I didn't want to believe Lauren was gone," Chum recalls from her blue living-room futon where she and Lauren would kick back on weekends. "When Lauren died, I went for a week without really knowing how to feel. My tears just came in waves. I couldn't stop crying at times. I was so stressed out and exhausted. I was sick to my stomach that first whole week."

When Chum and other CRU women cleaned out Lauren's dorm room, they gingerly removed the colorful drawings created by Lauren's little brother and sister—big sis loved to show off her siblings' handiwork. The women folded the blue-and-yellow patchwork quilt on Lauren's bed and gently tucked her photos of family and friends into boxes. Gut-wrenching emotions overcame Chum once again. She had to leave to vomit.

"The hardest thing for me was watching Chum terribly struggle over the loss of Lauren," shares Cynthia Thomas, the CRU staff woman who disciples Chum. "Chum is one of my gems, my star. She just loves Jesus so much and is always positive. To see her joy totally leave her was the worst part for me. Chum loved Lauren to death."

Lauren would understand Chum's distraught emotions and the sensitive stomach. After all, she is the one who vomited after praying to invite Jesus into her life. The three-year-old Lauren had been riding in the car with her mom when Lauren suddenly sat up straight and asked, "Have I ever asked Jesus into my heart?"

Sherry replied, "I haven't heard you. Would you like to now?" Mother and daughter prayed together thanking Jesus for his gift of eternal life and asking God to be real in Lauren's life. Little Lauren then fell asleep, but ten minutes later heaved all over the dashboard.

"I panicked at that point because I thought she would die and I would lose her," Sherry remembers. "I thought, *Why would Lauren ask me about Jesus and heaven right before she got sick?* For years I had a fear I would lose one of my children early. I talked to God about it, but I chose not to let myself dwell on this fear. Now I've realized my greatest fear, and God is still very good."

Still good to the McCains and Lauren's CRU family who await the continual unfolding of the tapestry of good that God is weaving from the dangling shreds of evil.

casey! Apr 17 2007 6:57ᴘ

myspace.com comment to Lauren McCain

you inspired so many because you lived like a real

Christian. your impact on so many lives, including my own, is astounding.

you really loved God and now you can finally dance before Him. i love you, lauren.

the lights will always "blink black" :)

9-28-06

If you didn't know, which you don't b/c I didn't write it down, I've been praying for a strong Christian friend to walk with me, someone to keep me accountable and encourage (mutually of course). Well, I went to the language partner meeting and I met a girl who knew Joel. Her name is Chum, and what a woman of God! Simply beautiful! She asked if I wanted to get coffee with her one morning just to talk, and knowing me, coffee + conversation = fun, so I said sure! We met later the next week and as we were talking I mentioned that Bible studies here were fun but very light. She agreed and explained that they didn't want to scare them away but she understood how I felt. Then out of the blue, she asked what I thought about discipling and I said, "Sounds cool!" So she offered to be my mentor, WOW! I got a close friend and mentor, all in one day. She's serious too, so no half-hearted seeking. (I'm happy!)

[From Lauren's journal]

CHAPTER FIVE

"THIS STINKS. THIS HURTS."

*This stinks. This hurts. There's no words
to describe what this feels like.*

—PASTOR DAVID BOUNDS, RESTORATION
CHURCH—PHOEBUS BAPTIST

The breaking news from Blacksburg interrupts the breakup headlines of Prince William's split with Kate Middleton. The Brits' romantic crumble thuds in stark contrast to the dead twentysomething Americans who will never even date again. And in early May, Prince William's grandmother, Queen Elizabeth II, visits the Commonwealth of Virginia for the four hundredth anniversary of Jamestown. Her straight-faced entourage of royal correctness starkly contrasts the raw, on-edge emotions of Virginia Tech's grieving.

Doreen Tomlin understands the intense churning of emotions while trying to grieve in the public eye. She lost her sixteen-year-old son, John, to the student gunmen at Columbine High School in 1999.

I can just feel the pain the Virginia Tech parents are going through. I watched the television reports from the Virginia campus, and finally I couldn't watch any more. As a parent who lost a child in the Columbine shootings, there's a tendency to go back into your own grief for a little while. I flashed back to what we went through. The wait to see if my son's name was on a list of those killed. The waiting was terrible. It took two days to find out for sure.

In the meantime, the media in your face is not fun. You lose a child to a disease and your grieving is private. But people really are clueless when you have a child murdered, and then the media plunges you into a different world. You are grieving, but a part of that grief is postponed with all the media attention. Our telephone rang nonstop for six weeks. "Can I have photographs of your child that no one else has?"

At times I feel like God picked me up by the collar of my shirt and held me over the ocean and dropped me in. That's a cold reflection of God, but at times that's how I felt. I didn't know how to deal with the cameras in our faces and all the phone calls.

While there is a coldness on the part of the media at times like this, I was also amazed how the Lord used the media to proclaim our faith. My prayer was for the greatest good to come from our loss, for people to know Jesus Christ through our words that went out to millions of people. And God answered that prayer.

I have special empathy and compassion for the Virginia Tech families in knowing that what they are walking through is just heart wrenching. On one hand you are filled with pain, and on the other there's an overwhelming sense of joy at how God is using your loss. Someone said to me, "You know it's God if those two extremes can exist within you at the same time."

Not a well-known destination for eager paparazzi, Blacksburg's carefree folk start counting the number of satellite-dish trucks parked around their college campus. With the media spotlight beaming intensely on this southwest Virginia university, some mourners like terror-stricken Molly Donohue nearly wilt—pressed to relive the chaos of April sixteenth in meaty sound bites to satiate the world's craving for instant, on-the-scene news. Tony Arnold, the media relations director for Campus Crusade's college ministries, drives up from his home in Cary, North Carolina, to Blacksburg. With essentially no room in any inn within twenty miles of campus, Tony crashes on the Highfields' couch.

"At first, all I knew was that Molly lived next door to the first murders and had discovered the bodies," Tony recalls. "I knew there would be an intense media frenzy to get to her."

Tuesday night at the International House of Pancakes in nearby Christiansburg, Virginia, Tony meets with Molly, her boyfriend, her parents, and her sister. Sarah Gale, the Campus Crusade's regional director for mid-Atlantic colleges, joins the group in a large booth in the crowded pancake parlor. As Blacksburg restaurants and coffee shops swarm with famished and stressed news teams—all waiting for more details to break in the bizarre murders—the IHOP on Peppers Ferry Road feels like a welcome oasis from the swirling chaos.

The IHOP tableside conversation eventually turns to the ultimate topic: What should Molly do about the media? Tony suggests a proactive approach—to talk with a select few of the national media outlets, then disappear. Molly's father restates the options to his weary daughter before letting Tony direct the conversation.

At this point the Donohues know few specifics of what their eighteen-year-old faced on the fourth floor of West AJ. Molly called home Monday to tell her parents that she was okay and was staying with off-campus friends. She asked her parents to join her for the Tuesday convocation, but mentioned nothing about witnessing the initial moments of Cho's first murders. Once her parents arrive and Molly does try to talk about the horrifying experience, she breaks down in tears and can't continue.

Tony warmly chats with Molly about growing up in Richmond, why she chose Virginia Tech, and how she got involved with CRU. After a few minutes of casual conversation, Tony lays the cards on the table: "Tell me about Monday morning."

The image of Molly sharing those painful details still troubles Tony:

Molly takes a deep breath and digs into her memory. Even though I am facing into the restaurant, everyone and everything behind Molly blurs out of my mind. Molly's mesmerizing words are also agonizing for all of us.

At one point, Molly's dad clears the dishes and condiments on the table separating him from Molly. With trembling hands and tears in his eyes, he grabs both of her hands and squeezes tight, sharing in her horror. This father is helpless to change what his daughter has endured.

I think of my own daughter in college and can identify with these parents' pain. Tears fill my own eyes numerous times as Molly relives her wakening moments from the day before.

Molly is both fragile and resilient. She's also a teenager, who, in the best of times, would probably rather hang out and have fun with her friends. Now, she struggles through a frightening fog of horrible memories.

Tony and the CRU family help shield Molly from the public eye. She stays with her Bible-study group at Dana Cox's the rest of the week. On Wednesday and Thursday, Molly's dedicated CRU friends accompany her to interviews with CBS, ABC, and NBC. These friends encircle Molly and pray her through the sobs and surreal recounting of being the first to witness Cho's bloody shoeprint stains so close to her own door.

In the days after the harrowing massacre, Tony and the Virginia Tech CRU team bolster their students with listening ears and an occasional game of freeze tag. One troubled junior asks Lisa Highfield for a favor: Would Jeff just give her a hug?

"The girl just wanted a big man, a big dad to hug her," Lisa explains. "Jeff gave her hugs throughout that first week and that really ministered to her."

The Virginia Tech students readily absorb the gestures of empathy, especially as their emotional numbness thaws and stinging questions poke to the surface.

"The university campus can become either a spiritual graveyard or a spiritual greenhouse. It's a place where a student's faith dies or blossoms," Tony Arnold explains. "The seeming randomness of the shootings in a dorm room and in a classroom building imbedded a fearful splinter into students' hearts and minds, 'It could have been me. It could have happened here. Is anyplace safe anymore?'"

With the rising tides of sorrow, both Christians and non-Christians ask the thorny questions: Where is God in all this? Why my friends, why our campus? How can I trust a God that would let this evil happen to so many innocent people?

Soul-penetrating questions. No pie-in-the-sky answers. Grief counselors and trauma experts advise university officials, local pastors, and staffers with student organizations like CRU to make themselves accessible to students, to get the distressed talking. Those who show intense signs of struggle are referred to professional counselors.*

"We can expect a full range of responses to this trauma. We are designed to ask questions and to problem-solve, and

---

*See the appendix for helpful answers to common post-trauma questions.

we are built to try to make sense of what has hurt us," explains Dr. Helen McIntosh, a psychologist who specializes in grief and trauma therapy and school-violence prevention.

"God longs for us to ask him for help and the grace to bear our pain, and to ask for the gift of trust until we can have wisdom to better understand our hurts. The real question is: Can we trust God to walk us through the valley of the shadow? The real answer is: God's grace that he has long promised, no matter the circumstances, no matter the size of our loss, no matter the damage we've experienced."

In his memorial message to the Virginia Tech mourners, Governor Tim Kaine reminded individuals to expect sadness and tears "by the boatload" and anger, maybe even despair. The governor relayed the story of Old Testament Job who railed at his Creator. "[Job] argued with God. He didn't lose his faith," Governor Kaine explained. "It's okay to argue. It's okay to be angry. Those emotions are natural as well. And finally . . . it can go beyond grief to isolation and feeling despair. Those haunting words that were uttered on a hill on Calvary: 'My God, My God, why have You forsaken Me?'"*

Feeling forsaken and entrenched in despair hit some grievers in little doses, then in overwhelming scoops.

---

*Matthew 27:46 (NKJV).

Others seemed to shut down their feelings altogether. When Dave and Sherry McCain hurried back to Hampton the eve of April 17, a sea of emotions swelled inside their two youngest ones as they learned that their beloved big sister would never come home again.

"We took them in our arms and told them Lauren was killed in a terrible accident with a bunch of other Tech students," Sherry says. "They were so angry and upset."

Ten-year-old Christian asked how his sister died, so his parents gently explained that she'd been shot. "They screamed and cried and yelled," Sherry adds. "And I was so glad they did." Dave and Sherry rocked their children and cried with them. That night, Abby slept with Sherry, and Dave couldn't sleep at all until after Lauren was brought back to Hampton.

Other children affected by the news of people hurt on campus reacted with their own questions and concerns. One night Jeff and Lisa Highfield's little daughter asked her parents at bedtime, "Why did the boy shoot those people?" Katie had pieced together details of the killer from television snippets and the conversations of CRU staff and students in their home.

"There's not too much training on how you tell a three-and-half-year-old about something like this," Jeff explains. "Lisa and I tried not to shield Katie totally and told her some in CRU got hurt. We tried to steer her mind from 'the boy' shooting people to praying for those who were still in the hospital."

At Blacksburg area schools, youth groups, and Sunday schools—even in classrooms in other states—teachers and helpers fielded questions from inquisitive and worried students. Sassie Duggleby, who coleads sixth through ninth graders at Northstar Church in Blacksburg, braced for the inevitable at youth group that first Wednesday night after the murders. A seventh grader immediately blurted, "Why would God do this?" For part of her response, Sassie read a copy of "Where Is God in the Midst of Tragedy?"*

"Our leaders talked with the kids about how we're not robots and God gives us a free will to make choices," Sassie explains. "Our kids in seventh grade were hit especially hard because three of their friends at school lost parents in the killings."

To her worried and questioning relatives and friends, Sassie zipped off an e-mail.

We have heard several stories that are amazing and show God was watching out for people. One student started walking toward Norris for class and his foot was really

---

*See the appendix for a copy of this article.

hurting, so he turned and went back to the dorm. He would have been in the classroom as the gunfire went off. Several told of sleeping in and skipping class that day, even though they usually attend. One professor has a weekly meeting on the second floor of Norris and for the first time all semester it was cancelled. I'm sure there are many more like that and they'll continue to pour in.

"God is our refuge and strength, an ever-present help in trouble. Therefore we will not fear, though the earth give way and the mountains fall into the heart of the sea, though its waters roar and foam and the mountains quake with their surging" (Psalm 46:1–3, NIV).

I trust that God is our refuge and strength in this time of trouble. Praise him that we do not have to fear!

As Sassie and others found, talking through misgivings and fears brings comfort and healing over time. Jim Pace, who helps to pastor New Life Christian Fellowship, a Virginia Tech church with roughly nine hundred attendees, found many students did want to express their sorrow, but only with a trusted few.

Pace talked to a number of students who hesitated to go too deep with "outsiders" because the students felt turned off by others "telling me what I am supposed to be thinking or feeling right now."

"The ugliness of this whole tragedy is difficult. We lost three of our students and Christians don't get a bye from the ugliness. The Earth is broken and we are subject to the same devastating events," Pace, a Hokie alumnus, explains. "For some, the shootings have shown them a need to get more serious spiritually. Others are going to go through this pretty angry at God. For others, this tragedy will blow up their faith unless we can help them see that we have a God that walks through the ugliness with us."

Cynthia Thomas's Campus Crusade for Christ Blog
April 20, 2007 *4:18 p.m.*
When it rains, it pours
Mark Gauthier, the national campus director, called us and gave us some very encouraging words from his heart and Scripture (wow!). . . . One thing he said that stuck out to me was, "For some reason, God has chosen to point a spotlight on Virginia Tech for all the world to see." Ugh, ain't that the truth.

I confess kind of loathing that truth, but at the same time I am very intrigued at what God is doing, and what he will do as a result of the massive amounts of prayer that are going up for us right now. Also, historically, persecution and difficulty have never been a bad thing for the church. It is in these times when

Christianity explodes and we are forced to sink or swim. I am anxious to see what God will do here through this time, and around the world. I can't see much of that now, but I am trusting by faith that I will.

By faith, those who follow God are edging forward in their beliefs despite the temptation to make wrong assumptions and wrong conclusions about their Creator and why some of his creations died at the hand of one ill student. One of these believers is Andrea Kebede, a Virginia Tech English major who graduated a month after the shootings and is dearly missing three of her slain friends.

Monday afternoon as we waited to get news on who was killed, I remember praying, *Lord, I just want to make sure I'm on the right standing with you right now. This guy could come back and I don't know how safe I am. I just don't know.* So, around five o'clock, I decided to go to a vigil held by Chi Alpha, a Christian organization on campus.

That's where I found out that one of my friends had died. His name is Ryan Clark. He was an RA in West AJ. That news was horrific! *Why him?* Even just thinking about it now just blows my mind, because

I had just seen Ryan. We used to study together and he was extremely bright and kind. He always asked, "Are you okay?" And he sincerely wanted to know.

Then I found out that yet another guy, Brian Bluhm, who attended BCM (Baptist Collegiate Ministries), was killed. That was another major blow. I was angry and asking, "Why?" I've never really dealt with so much death at once before.

I needed to stay around strong Christians at this time, so I called my friends, Pastor Bob and Sandra Jackson, and asked if could stay with them. They immediately opened their home and hearts to me.

My tears didn't start coming until Wednesday. My tears came in spurts, and then I had headaches from all the tension. I felt like I should be bawling, but I couldn't. I just felt numb.

Later in the week, I found out a third friend, Nicole White, had passed. I didn't know what to do at that point. I was seriously overwhelmed. I remember Nicole when she was a freshman and I was a sophomore. We had grown into a more intimate relationship than Brian and Ryan and I.

Again, I was angry, not so much at God, but angrily asking, "How could such a person like this be killed?" None of this felt fair. I was asking God, "Where is justice in all this?"

That week, and even now, I have to keep going back to a Bible verse God showed me at the Chi Alpha prayer vigil, Isaiah 61:2–3, ". . . To comfort all who mourn, to grant those who mourn in Zion, giving them a garland instead of ashes, the oil of gladness instead of mourning, the mantle of praise instead of a spirit of fainting so they will be called oaks of righteousness, the planting of the Lord, that He may be glorified (NASB).

As soon at I read this verse at the vigil, I heard a CD playing in the background with the words to this Scripture. God was definitely speaking to me!

I have not struggled with forgiveness in all this, my difficulty comes in the "Why? Why *my* people? Why *my* three friends?" So I keep clinging to God and his Word as my questions and grief come and go. I trust that God will give me "gladness instead of mourning."

Hey, 10-30-06

Teach me your ways, that I may know you and find favor in your sight! Ex.33:13 Do this! I want to know you, to be intimate with you! I'm seeking you so help me to be disciplined and focused. Even when the excitement is gone let there still be a passionate (or loving) commitment on my part to find and understand you. Let my joy be in understanding and _knowing_ you. Redeem (or teach me to) the time so that it's fruitful. My eyes are on you, but I'm human and my heart is very wayward. But God, I desire you! I want to find you and be found in you! So teach me your ways so that I'll know you. Thank you for delighting in me, thank you for not letting me stay in one place longer than necessary. Take my life, take it! Lol, I'm yours, and you are mine!

—Lauren

[Notes from Lauren's Bible study]

CHAPTER SIX

I CAN ONLY IMAGINE

*I can only imagine . . . how wonderful
heaven will be.*

—LAUREN MCCAIN, IN HER FRIEND AMY'S
TWENTY-FIRST BIRTHDAY CARD

Thirty-six-year-old Mark Stremler takes a sip of his Boston Beanery coffee and clutches the thick mug as if its warmth will melt a mental block in his head. He's a Virginia Tech regular at the just-off-campus restaurant, and today the associate professor of engineering science and mechanics settles back in his booth. He's in no rush to get back to his office.

Mark's gaze darts out the window toward Norris Hall. The realization of what really happened right below his office on the morning of April 16 make it difficult to begin.

His silence stretches into nearly a minute. He remembers the awful sounds. Finally the words come about that terrifying morning.

My office is in Norris—309, on the third floor right above 211, the French classroom. On my drive through campus that Monday morning, I see a bunch of police outside AJ. I figure they'd caught the person calling in bomb threats over the last several weeks. I reach my office a little before 9:00 A.M. and started writing on a paper. I plan to stay at my computer until 9:45, when I need to drop off some library books before a 10:10 meeting.

Since there's a class across the hall, I close my door to keep out the sounds of students coming and going. At 9:29 I receive the e-mail about a shooting and to report suspicious activity to the police. Not giving it much thought, I keep typing. About ten to fifteen minutes later I hear loud banging. It sounds like someone pounding a sledgehammer against sheet metal.

The sounds are so methodical. Bang . . . Bang . . . Bang . . . Bang . . . Bang. The yelling starts and has a panicked edge to it. I look out the window and hear a distinct yell of "Gun!" That's when I realize that the bangs are gunshots. I see a man in a suit walk out of Burruss Hall, but someone yells at him and he darts back inside.

I open my door and see students from the classroom across the hall going into Kevin Granata's office,

311, next to mine. Kevin must have just passed my door before I open it. He heads downstairs to see what is going on and if he can help, I suppose. But he doesn't come back.

Mark stops. Blinks. Squints his eyes. The vacant stare settles in. The silence lingers once again.

"I keep wondering: If I opened my door a minute earlier, would I have stopped Kevin from going down to the second floor? Or would I have gone down with him?" Mark says, scooting his mug away from the table's edge. "I really don't know. It could have gone either way."

I lock myself in my office. I'm not sure if bullets are hitting the ceiling below me, but I can feel the vibrations on my office floor making this surreal situation more real. I see a SWAT officer approaching Norris, and my hands start to shake as the danger sinks in. I hear sirens. I think about my family, my wife, and four kids. I pray, asking for the shooting to stop, for God to protect me . . . to protect all of us.

Finally the gunfire ends. I hear the police yelling down the hall and banging on the doors. I open my door to three guns in my face. The officers make sure I am not armed, then send me running—my hands up—down a stairwell and outside to the Drillfield. The campus is locked down, and I end up in the War Memorial Gym. I borrow a graduate student's cell phone and call my wife at work.

The professor who relishes theoretical and applied mechanics pauses again. He thinks of losing his department friends, Liviu Librescu and Kevin Granata, in the murderous mayhem. A minute later, Mark changes the subject and talks of his children—two girls and two boys ranging in age from eleven to five years old. He shares how the shootings impress upon him to pray more conscientiously for his children and to spend more daily time together with his family. But soon he goes back to the shootings. Mark admits he's been more on edge and watches his temper flare more readily. He understands it's part of the recovery process for post-traumatic stress disorder. He's tried to journal his experience, too, but never gets too far.

I find myself sitting somewhere or out running when suddenly I flash back to that morning. I lose track of where I am physically as I go back to Norris Hall in my mind, replaying scenarios of what I could have done differently. God protected me well, I was never in immediate danger on April 16. I just have the memories of hearing the gunshots and feeling the vibrations.

The tragedy makes clear the importance of my faith. . . . You never know what tomorrow holds, so you need to make sure that you take care of today. I've also been reminded that life isn't always easy.

I'm not really asking "Why God?" so much. My biggest question is: What should I have done differently? Logically, if I had gone to the second floor, there is a good chance I would have been killed, too. Emotionally, though, my thoughts are: *What if? What if I had gone down to the second floor with Kevin? What if there had been one more person down there? Could something different have happened?*

Attending Liviu's and Kevin's memorial services helped. So did walking back into Norris to get some things from his office. "I stopped by Kevin's and Liviu's offices," Mark adds. "It gave me a chance to say good-bye."

For now, this engineering colleague relives the haunting, helpless moments of listening to the handgun rampage below his office. And when Mark wonders what he could have done to intervene—he pauses, and turns those thoughts toward heaven.

. . .

One wonders if Lauren McCain, who called her college campus a "slice of heaven," slipped past the praying Professor Stremler on her way to her divine home. She died in Room 207, just feet below Mark.

Those who knew and loved Lauren now find solace and peace in the courageous yet comforting words she shared in her final months of life. For close high-school friend Amy Yates's twenty-first birthday, February 12, 2007, Lauren penned the following in Amy's birthday card:

Amy,

My wonderful sister in Christ! I am so glad that God has allowed me to grow with you and glorify him together. Being away has been hard, but every time I get down, I know that you care for me and that no matter what, you love me.

On your big 21st I want to remind you how good our God is. How he uses all things to glorify himself, which in turn is good for us. I pray that he will continue to grow you into his image. I can only imagine . . . how wonderful heaven will be. But until then I will always be praying for you and growing with you. As much as I love you, I

know God does, too, even more (as impossible as that
sounds). So I commit you to him and ask that we'll have
more than 21 more years to continue growing together.

   ❤ *Lauren*

   Happy Birthday

In early 2007, Lauren could only imagine how wonderful heaven would be. On April 16 she knew, with nothing of God's wonders left to her imagination. Ten days
after Amy's birthday, Lauren records more insights about
heaven. On a wind-whipped February 22, Campus Crusade films Lauren in a personal interview about finding
eternal life and living in God's power. The ministry's aim
is to talk to a number of college Christians nationwide
about their faith, and the local Virginia Tech CRU staff
recommends the articulate freshman. Sporting a favorite
jean jacket and brown bead necklace, Lauren answers the
interview questions with confidence:

In the Bible, it says in Joel 2:32, "but whoever calls on
the name of the Lord will be saved." It's kind of like a
promise that he gives us, and when Christ was on the
cross, and the sinner was beside him . . . and he was
confessing that, ah, you are Lord, you know, I believe. And Christ said, "[T]oday you'll be in paradise

with me" [Luke 23:43, NIV]. So, as soon as you accept Christ, Christ is like, this is what it is. . . .

God promises us joy and peace and that's something that he gives us that's supernatural. It's not something that's from within, so much as something that he gives to us through his Holy Spirit, and through his promises. That we can have peace that what he says is true, and that we have joy that we're going to live in heaven, and that we're going to walk with him on Earth. . . .

It says through Scripture that we will be in "Paradise" with him . . . and even now as he's sitting at the right hand of God, our lives are with him. So, I guess in a sense, technically we're there.

Listening to Lauren speak truths about heaven brings to mind a blessed assurance that Jesus was the central focus of this twenty-year-old's life. After the interview, Lauren tells her mother, "Guess what? I didn't even wear makeup. I wanted the interview to be all about Christ and not about me."

Typical Lauren. Naturally beautiful with an independent streak. Sherry remembers Lauren as a little girl stubbornly wanting her way in life.

"I'd tell Lauren her hair was pretty today, and she'd

stomp off mad as a hornet. She thought I meant it was ugly the rest of the time," Sherry explains, with a nostalgic fondness. "I just didn't get Lauren when she was little. She used to throw fits and couldn't deal with her own anger. Lauren was the epitome of the strong-willed child, a mom's nightmare.

"God gave me the word picture that Lauren was a diamond, and I had to guide her and teach her to love him so her strength would be strong for his glory. I prayed for insight to raise Lauren and appreciate her. I asked God for the eyes to see her as a blessing. And he answered my prayers!"

As lively Lauren moved into her teen years, her intense emotions softened. She played soccer full throttle and cherished laughter with her friends. Lauren liked boys, but dating and finding Mr. Right never topped her A-list. At Virginia Tech, Lauren hung out with her male buddies, but chose to concentrate more on helping international students learn English—or select toppings for their sub sandwiches.

. . .

Phillip Zellner met Lauren in their church youth group as teenagers and stayed close buds through the years. Lauren joined Phillip at Virginia Tech, and he is quick to point out

Lauren's strengths. "You couldn't talk to Lauren without it making you want to be better," Phillip explains. "She was so on fire for God, it made you want to love God, too. Even if she was having a bad day, she would still just talk to you like you were the only person in the world."

Phillip chuckles when he thinks about Lauren's not-so-stong suits. "Lauren would just forget where she put her phone, her keys, lots of things. She was also directionally challenged and couldn't tell north from south," the senior in electrical engineering adds. "There are so many times she called me up in class because she was lost."

When it came to setting her priorities, Lauren was anything but lost. She kept an active social schedule with both her guy and gal friends, but didn't major in "boy crazy" like some women her age.

"People got it in their minds that Lauren determined she wasn't ever going to get married. It so wasn't true," Amy shares. "One night we went back to Lauren's house and had fun with her mom picturing each of our husbands. Marriage definitely wasn't out of the question, it just wasn't for us right now."

When she was seventeen, Lauren's father took his oldest daughter on her first date. They ate at Olive Garden, attended a concert, then topped the evening off with coffee at Starbucks.

"Sherry made me leave the house and come back and knock on the door," Dave says, wanting to treat his daughter like she should expect every man to treat her. "Lauren was all dressed up. The server at dinner asked Lauren if she wanted to try the wine, and we both just died laughing."

Dave stops, his voice cracks. Memories of his precious daughter mean more these days than they ever have.

A quick study for foreign languages, Lauren dreamed of someday working overseas and representing God to her coworkers and all those whom God placed in her path. Lauren preferred to move with an everyday vocation and not as a missionary worker.

When she turned eighteen, Lauren celebrated her birthday with Katelyn Macri; their birthdays were a month apart. Katelyn wanted everyone to come as what they would be in twenty years. Lauren dressed as death, all in black—complete with darkened veil. Their birthday-party friends freaked at her morbid sense of humor. Lauren asked, "Why are you so upset? If I'm not here in twenty years, you know where I'm going to be."

Uncanny? Maybe. Prophetic? Perhaps. The college freshman did not seem to fear her own immortality. Lauren overflowed with an impassioned desire to live loudly and to let her life resonate into the lives of others for eternity. No doubt, her desire is coming true.

"I've had several people tell me she lived a full life. When you look at it in eternity spectrum, she's still alive. She's not dead. She just graduated. She went home early. She spited me. She's not going to pick my retirement home," Dave adds with a chuckle. "Lauren didn't die of a long, debilitating disease, she was not in a coma for months and months. The very worst thing for us is the very best thing for her. Lauren's desires were to see God and to share his love around the world; she's done both of those."

Dave and Sherry McCain believe God was not absent from the classroom the morning Lauren died. They feel Lauren's life—and death—fit perfectly into God's plan.

"Lauren's job was done. It was time for her to be home. She's run her race, she has her reward. Look at it in the light of eternity. This is the best place for her to be," Sherry says with intensity. "It's hard for us. We only have to mourn that we don't have her here. God has left us nothing else to mourn. That is huge. Lauren was ready for heaven. Even by her own testimony, she was ready."

For instance, we know that when these bodies of ours are taken down like tents and folded away, they will be replaced by resurrection bodies in heaven—God-made, not handmade—and we'll never have to relocate our "tents" again. Sometimes we can hardly wait to move—and so we cry out in frustration. Compared to what's coming, living conditions around here seem like a stop-over in an unfurnished shack, and we're tired of it! We've been given a glimpse of the real thing, our true home, our resurrection bodies! The Spirit of God whets our appetite by giving us a taste of what's ahead. He puts a little of heaven in our hearts so that we'll never settle for less.

—2 CORINTHIANS 5:1–5 (TM)

"The Bible in 2 Corinthians 5 talks about us being in earthly tents, but in heaven it will be the sweetest time when we're in the presence of God. God is using even the loss of Lauren to grow me so much," says Leah Mummert, a close friend and Hampton church buddy. "I just have a picture of Lauren in heaven: She's so overwhelmed with joy that you can't help but laugh or cry. God is working through the fear of death showing me it's not that scary, and it's the most awesome thing ever. We're here just waiting in line."

⁓

11-7-06

Search me, Oh God, and know my heart; try me and know my anxious thoughts and see if there be any hurtful way in me, and lead me in the everlasting way. Psalm 139:23–24 Anxious thoughts are huge for me. I worry about friends, happiness, school, fitness. I loved when we talked about being humble enough to give all my thoughts to you. So, how much more should I give these burdened thoughts up? I can get pretty miserable when I try to fix them, or just dwell on them. Especially the having friends part. So, I'm giving them to you, and I will trust you to do whatever or lead me to do whatever. Love you!

    —Lauren

[Notes from Lauren's Bible study]

CHAPTER SEVEN
HOPE FOR THE HELPLESS

*We are humbled by this darkness. We feel
hopeless, helpless, and lost. . . .*

—SUN-KYUNG CHO, SISTER OF SEUNG-HUI CHO

Four days after Seung-Hui Cho rips through his cocoon of silence with malicious gunfire, his family releases a written statement of their unspeakable anguish. Friday, April 20, is the same day people throughout Virginia, and across America, wear Hokie maroon and orange to remember the slain. At noon, church bells toll nationwide, while silence muffles the Virginia Tech campus.

"This is someone that I grew up with and loved. Now I feel like I didn't know this person. . . ." writes Cho's sister, Sun-Kyung, on behalf of her family. "We never could have envisioned that he was capable of so much violence.

"He has made the world weep. We are living a nightmare."

This nightmare awakens mourners worldwide to the stinging reality of mass murder that ends in suicide. Individuals stunned by the abhorrent massacre ponder the fleetingness of life. The lesson for many: Life is short. The indelible message for Christians in particular: Make each day count fully. Live strong for God.

Lauren McCain would have it no other way.

Those who lift their eyes from the bitter ashes of loss and grief are now catching glimpses of God's ever-steady grace and hope. Many see God's presence even in the terrifying minutes of that April morning.

While Cho still clutches his handguns in violent defiance, his targets are praying. So are countless others in the rest of the building. While the bullets zip and bodies crumple, police officers scramble up the stairs of Norris Hall.

Soon emergency medical teams compress bleeding arteries. Nurses administer medicine to ease throbbing wounds. Doctors pump silent chests hoping to revive those who are already gone.

Pastors, counselors, and concerned citizens gather to offer a hand to squeeze, an ear to listen. Most words fall inadequate against the tide of confusion and distress. Another box of tissues, another tight embrace. Through it all, Virginia Tech refuses to surrender its will and its resilience.

Sun-Kyung Cho expresses that her family feels "hope-less, helpless, and lost." They are not alone in the despera-tion. They are not alone in the search for answers. Yet hope and help arise bit by bit to ease the despondent and aimless feelings within.

. . .

"Often the first thing I think of when someone loses a child is that God has been there, too. He lost his only son. God imparts an amazing empathy and understanding, not just because he is God, but because he personally knows sorrow himself," says Massachusetts psychologist Dr. Julie Cox.

"And the Bible talks in 1 Thessalonians 4:13, '[D]o not grieve as those who have no hope' [NIV]. This verse ac-tually implies, 'Yes, go ahead and grieve, but your grief doesn't have to be the kind that has no hope of ever seeing your loved one again.' If you know that your child was a believer, and you are as well, God promises in no uncer-tain terms that you will be together again."

It's the unshakable promise that Dave and Sherry McCain and other mourning parents hold to in their whirl-wind of loss . . . and in their longing to see their sons' and daughters' smiles once again.

From his College of Agriculture and Life Sciences office at Virginia Tech, Joe Guthrie reflects on the hope and help he sees emerging from the immense loss. Both a man who knows his cattle breeds and a man who knows his God, Joes claps his hands and studies his office's cream cinder-block walls. The agricultural technology instructor sports a "Beef. It's What's for Dinner." sticker on the top drawer of his Latham Hall file cabinet. He works to pull up the chaotic events of the week he will never forget.

"Cho's mind-set was to rip this place apart, to destroy this campus," Joe says. "But instead of destroying us, he's made us stronger."

Monday morning as news of the shootings spreads across campus, slender-framed Joe stands guard over Latham Hall exit doors informing fidgety agricultural students that they cannot leave the building. Tuesday, as a trained pastoral counselor, Joe hooks up with the American Red Cross and offers his listening ear to distraught and grieving families huddling at the Inn. He passes out food and drinks to the hurting, but doesn't take time to eat himself all day.

"In a lot of ways the evil we saw is already being overcome with good," Joe explains. "Together we've shed a lot of tears, but we've expressed a lot of love, too. While there will never be enough good that comes from this to overcome the deaths, you can't help but see the good already happening here."

A graduate of Virginia Tech himself, the professor-cattleman picks up on the good in the outpouring of the university community and those from afar who come to serve the hurting. He also observes the good in the "Hokie Stone" memorials, (basketball-sized rocks that resemble the gorgeous Hokie stone buildings on campus) placed in a half-circle on the knoll of the Drillfield.

Gifts of fresh-cut flowers, stuffed animals, burning candles, and personal notes stack up around white slips of paper with the typed name of each person slain. From Ross Abdallah Alameddine to Nicole White, with Jarrett Lane, Lauren McCain, and Mary Read in the middle.

"The memorials are another way the university community is saying, 'we remember,'" adds Joe. "There are few things that are more helpful to the families than knowing that their child or loved one is remembered, and that their lives were significant."

Local businesses donate chicken sandwiches, pizzas, and more to help feed the masses of CRU and other students meeting for prayer and worship. Some on campus distribute a sheet of printed prayers. Other visitors near the War Memorial Chapel give away bottles of water, apples, and chips to passersby, along with CDs and full-color booklets about finding God in times of crisis.

A team of volunteers from across the country fly and drive their affectionate dogs to Blacksburg so students strolling across campus can pause to pet, hug, and kiss these canine companions. There's comfort in fluffy fur and warm slobbers. Another man outside the student center sits playing an upright piano out of the tiny back end of a well-used pickup. There's healing in the sounds of music.

In the remaining days of the school year, dozens of Christ followers—students, university employees, and campus visitors—join together every noon on the steps near Norris Hall to lift up their voices in praise and prayer to God. Despite their sorrow, these faithful lift their eyes toward the skies and away from the state police cars and yellow crime-scene tape some fifty yards away.

. . .

While the Hokies do unite, the temptation is to be noble "fixers," to right the horrible wrong inflicted on some of America's finest students and academics. Or to rush through the process of grieving, or to medicate the pain with a litany of unhealthy, soul-numbing choices. Alcohol.

Busyness. Drugs. Food. Some vow to never speak of the horror again.

"It's essential to make room for people to grieve and talk about their feelings and reminisce about the person they've lost. But one of the most unhelpful things is when families with such profound grief are unsure what to do with their sorrow, so they just stop talking about their loved one," notes Dr. Cox.

"They almost pretend like the person who died never existed. While trying to remove the sadness, they often lose the memories of joy this person brought into their lives. Joy and sorrow go together."

Seasoned caregivers, like Dr. Cox and Joe Guthrie, understand sorrow carving into one's being and making room for joy. They also know to follow the model of Jesus when his close friend, Lazarus, dies. Jesus sobs. It's the Bible's shortest verse, John 11:35 (NIV).

"Jesus wept."

To the hurting and helpless, these two words may be the Bible's most profound.

The wise and sensitive among the caregivers also realize that many mourners' circles of support stop listening long before the grievers stop talking. As the rest of the country anticipates the next *American Idol* winner or clamors over the latest goofy clips on YouTube.com, the lamenting of Virginia Tech find their tragedy somehow slipping through the cracks of yesterday's news.

"Our culture is so crisis-oriented, and we see something on the news for a day or two and then it's gone," says Dr. Cox. "The crisis is over for the rest of America, but in the meantime it's not over for the suffering, even if we don't see the images on TV anymore."

That's when Dr. Cox recommends the community around the grievers—extended family, neighbors, church family—to love, love, *love* in tangible ways.

That can sound like: *Do you need some time alone or time to go for a walk? I'll babysit the kids for an hour so you can go do that. Do you need to go to the gravesite? Do you want to go by yourself or should I come with you?*

"There's a wonderful scene in *Broadcast News*," says Dr. Cox, "where Albert Brooks loses his job and he's really distressed and says to a friend he's known for years. 'I need to be alone.' The friend replies, 'Okay. I'll go with you.' There are times when the grieving need to be alone, but this movie scene shows the kind of love and sensitivity all hurting people need. We must never forget there are walking wounded among us. The hurting of Virginia Tech are living in a wake of grief that the majority of us just can't imagine."

Wading through the wake of grief, the Virginia Tech

CRU family gathers again, April 19, for their regular Thursday night meeting in Squires Student Center. In a special tribute to Jarrett, Mary, and Lauren, the group shares what they appreciate and will miss the most about their fallen friends.

The memorial slide presentation elicits many tears, some smiles, and even a chuckle or two. Senior Jarrett Lane is remembered for his fun-loving spirit and perpetual influence as a friend and mentor.

A note is read from Mary's parents describing how she loved being a part of Campus Crusade and her Bible study. The card shares how her five younger siblings adored Mary—each wanting to be just like big sis. The weekend before she died, Mary was back home sitting on the stairs IMing her friends on her laptop. Her little brother snuggled next to her, clicking away at a toy computer in his lap.

Lauren's little brother and sister adored her, too. So did her CRU friends, as evidenced by their words of remembrance that first Thursday night after her home-going:

"Lauren challenged me to know Scripture more."

"The reason God took her is because he wanted her back.
But I feel so selfish because
I want her back here."

"Somehow when you talked to Lauren, she got to the center of your soul."

"I was mad at God, like, 'God, she could have totally rocked this campus for you!' And then I thought, 'Wow! She already has.'"

12-14-06

Equip me to fight the good fight at school. Bring warriors alongside me, to encourage me and for me to encourage! Then open the ministry and good works you've prepared for us to be faithful in from the beginning!

Smooth out the edges that have been chipped off this semester!

Form me into your image and use me however pleases you most. Don't let me waste this time.

[From Lauren's journal]

CHAPTER EIGHT
I FORGIVE YOU

*. . . Even though I hurt to the core; even
though my eyes are tired of crying; even
though campus, my home, will never
be the same . . . I forgive you. . . .*

—NOTE LEFT ON CHO'S MEMORIAL STONE

When the urge for revenge seeps into her heart, Doreen Tomlin thinks about Dutch Holocaust survivor Corrie ten Boom. Doreen lost her sixteen-year-old, John, to the bullets of Columbine. Corrie lost her sister, Betsie, to the brutality of Ravensbrük.

After her release in 1944, Corrie spots the Nazi officer responsible for much of the abuse Betsie and she endured. The man says he is now a Christian and asks for Corrie's forgiveness. He extends his hand. Corrie recoils.

Her heart cringes at the idea of letting this murderer off the hook. The Spirit nudges. Corrie resists. Slowly the former concentration camp prisoner offers her hand in a sign of reluctant obedience. Corrie chooses to offer pardon to this killer even though the very idea chafes against her emotions.

"Corrie ten Boom set an example for me," Doreen Tomlin shares. "At times I felt some bitterness and I didn't feel like forgiving Dylan and Eric. I'd get angry on and off when I saw their pictures on TV practicing shooting, and I'd think, *Yeah, that was my son's head!* I had to keep praying for God to help me forgive. We're supposed to emulate what God would do, but that didn't come overnight for me. I really rest in the fact that I don't feel vengeful because God will be their judge."

Noted British author and scholar C. S. Lewis once said, "Everyone says forgiveness is a lovely idea until they have something to forgive." Forgiving Cho for his brutal assault on so many unsuspecting people is not a lovely idea. Neither is forgiving the questionable systems that some blame for allowing Cho to commit his heinous acts in the first place.

"Forgiveness" does sound so lovely. So easy. So simple to roll off the tongue in a nippy three-syllable blurt. Yet, as time drones on and bleeding hearts either mend or crust over, unforgivingness roars its despicable head.

Unforgivingness never dies young. Unforgiveness issues can fester for years, locking its victims in bitterness and rage.

Must we remember the thirty-third person who dies

that blustery April morning? Must we remember—and forgive—someone whose inner loathing explodes in blazing murder? Must we pardon an unbalanced young man who sacrifices so many in the crosshairs of his own rage? Must we?

For those who claim the way of the Savior, life eventually propels them into the defining crossroads. Choose the way of the cross or choose the way of self. Follow in the footsteps of the Master and turn the other cheek, or walk away in blame and ill will. In first-century Israel, Jesus Christ speaks these words that still resonate to the core of Christianity: "Do not judge, and you will not be judged. Do not condemn, and you will not be condemned. Forgive, and you will be forgiven" (Luke 6:37, NIV).

No judging, no condemning, just forgiving. Yet God doesn't expect his children to muster up forgiveness on their own, particularly when brutal offenses like murder tear into their lives. For it was the agonizing man at Calvary who uttered his final words before death, "Father, forgive them, for they do not know what they are doing" (Luke 23:34, NIV).

He's also the one who promised his followers, "But the Counselor, the Holy Spirit, whom the Father will send in my name, will teach you all things and will remind you of everything I have said to you" (John 14:26, NIV). Everything including forgiveness.

CRU students Lauren, Jarrett, and Mary encourage Jesus' radical forgiveness long before their lives tragically end. Their message of forgiveness reverberates louder than the gunshots in the rooms where they are killed. Molly Donohue, who studied the Bible every week with Lauren in West Ambler Johnston, is choosing to model forgiveness like Jesus and Lauren.

"I can't think of any point where I didn't feel forgiveness toward the gunman. My first reaction was to forgive, and I couldn't deal with the emotion of holding a grudge," Molly says, still reeling from discovering the murder scene in her dorm. "Lauren probably was praying for Cho as he was shooting in the classroom. I forgave him because I knew that Lauren would have."

In *The Tragedy of King Richard the Second*, William Shakespeare penned, "I pardon him as God shall pardon me." In picking up the shattered pieces of what was once a typical college life, many Virginia Tech students, like Molly, focus less on pardoning the gunman and more on how God pardons them.

· · ·

People loved to listen to Lauren's worshipful prayers. Here, Lauren prays at the Campus Crusade for Christ Bridges Conference in Houston, Texas. *Photo courtesy of Campus Crusade for Christ*

Lauren adored her great-grandmother Fern Martin.

Photo by Sherry McCain

Joel, Abby, Lauren, and Christian McCain goofing around during summer vacation 2006. *Photo by Sherry McCain*

Lauren and her close friend Amy Yates at Amy's surprise twenty-first birthday party.
Photo courtesy of the McCain Family

Lauren and some friends from Bridges International.
Photo by Blair Pippin

Lauren and her Bible-study friends, Janelle Frasier, Dana Cox, and Sarah Olmstead, on the ropes course at the 2006 CRU fall retreat at Rockbridge Alum Springs Camp, near Lexington, Virginia.

Photo courtesy of Campus Crusade for Christ

Freshman Bible-study members Janelle Frasier, Molly Donohue, Sarah Olmstead, and Lauren with some male friends at the CRU Christmas party in December 2006. *Photo courtesy of Campus Crusade for Christ*

Lauren and her Bridges mentor, Chum Hoang, in the kitchen where they cooked on Friday nights for Virginia Tech international students. *Photo courtesy of Chum Hoang*

One of the many makeshift memorials placed around the Virginia Tech campus. *Photo courtesy of Getty Images*

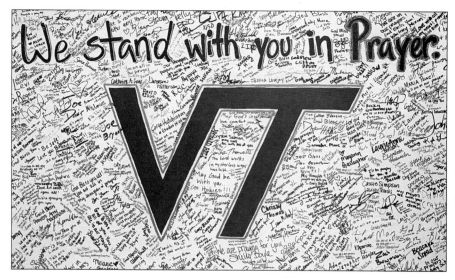

A memorial banner for the slain Virginia Tech students and professors. *Photo courtesy of Getty Images*

A Virginia Tech student praying at an interdenominational memorial service. *Photo courtesy of Getty Images*

One of the last photos of Lauren, snapped by her father during Easter weekend 2007. *Photo by Dave McCain*

"I'm sad that the gunman was disturbed and hurt and in pain for so much of his life. But for our own sanity, we have to forgive this man or he will continue to hold power over us, as will Satan," explains Cynthia Thomas, who oversees the women in Lauren and Molly's Bible-study chain.

"The longer I allow unforgivingness to reign in my heart, the more I'm focusing on the gunman and not on my friends who died. Or on the living that need my help right now. What the killer did *is* a big deal, but in God's eyes, my sin is equal to his sin. I'm just as much in need of a Savior as Cho was."

No one but the Almighty seems to be clear on where Cho stood in his own spiritual life and in his own beliefs on God's forgiveness.

Young-Hwan Kim, a twenty-four-year-old civil engineering student, is president of the Korean Campus Crusade for Christ (KCCC) group at Virginia Tech. With some one hundred thirty students of South Korean descent in their chapter, Young-Hwan explains that most Korean international students at Virginia Tech study engineering, math, or science, so they would not naturally interact with English major Cho. But Young-Hwan believes his group made efforts to reach out to Cho at some point.

Every year KCCC gets a list of freshmen who are coming to Virginia Tech. The group sends out e-mails inviting the new students to the KCCC weekly meeting and fun activities. Group members also visit door-to-door inviting other Korean students to attend.

"I don't know, somehow we lost contact with this Seung-Hui Cho. Maybe he refused to join our group," Young-Hwan Kim says. "At Virginia Tech there are about sixteen hundred Asian students, so maybe we stopped e-mailing him, or maybe he ignored those e-mails and refused to join our group . . . unfortunately."

Also unfortunately, no one on Earth knows for sure why loner Cho apparently turned from his church upbringing and slipped further into a cavern of spiritual darkness. His childhood pastor at Korean Presbyterian Church, in Centreville, Virginia, tells *Newsweek* that "Cho was a smart student who could understand the meaning of the Bible . . . and [his] prayers were always short, very short."

Pastor Hyun David Chung, senior pastor of Korean Baptist Church of Blacksburg, who leads a congregation of about one hundred fifty Virginia Tech students, prefers not to speak the killer's Korean name. He refers to Cho as "this guy."

"So far as I know, while this guy was in Blacksburg, he was never involved in any kind of Christian activity. He was not part of our church," Pastor David says. "There are a lot of Asian Christian groups, but none of these groups that I know had any chance to talk to him or knew him personally. So, virtually no one knew him."

On campus and in the Blacksburg community, few know little if anything about Seung-Hui Cho. Practically nothing until he leaves his calling cards in West AJ and Norris Hall.

Now the world knows more about the alienated Cho than even his own family or his dorm suitemates did before the shootings. Now Cho's name tops the list of America's deadliest assassins on a high-school or college campus, or any other place—public or private.

In 1966, at the University of Texas in Austin, a student in a ninety-six-minute homicidal rage kills sixteen people and wounds thirty-one. He had murdered his wife and mother the night before. Ten years later, a custodian fatally shoots seven fellow employees and wounds two others at California State University, Fullerton. Skip ahead another twenty years to 1996, and a San Diego State graduate student, while defending his thesis, pulls a handgun and kills three professors.

The alarming homicides at Virginia Tech are not the first to startle the nation, nor, unfortunately, will they be the last. But somewhere in the chaos, as the gun smoke drifts away, God's people are taking a stand. They are standing up for the sacredness of life . . . and death.

On Sunday, April 22, less than a week after the campus shootings, Pastor Bob Jackson of Blacksburg guides his worshippers through a time of both somber reflection and personal challenge. Pastor Bob, who leads Northstar Church, calls the Virginia Tech tragedy a "forced pause."

"In the normal routine of our hyper-busyness and overly scheduled lives, we rarely take the time to ponder the large issues of existence—where we are headed, why we are headed there," Pastor Bob notes. "Unless we are interrupted, or choose to interrupt ourselves, we may not pause to look at what is wrong with our lives, as well as what is right, and how our relationship with God is going. Something like this horrific event can force us into that kind of self-examination, which I believe can be very healthy."

Healthy but still difficult, as Lauren's close friend from Hampton and Virginia Tech, Phillip Zellner, knows.

I still haven't seen Cho's video clips. I don't know if I will, if I even care to. I struggle with two competing things: On one hand, I don't want to dismiss the shootings like nothing ever happened. On the other, I have to forgive Cho because Jesus said anyone can love their friends, but he's called us to love our enemies as well.

The enemy isn't even Cho. We don't mess with flesh and blood. Cho was a tool that Satan used to cause destruction. Fortunately, God showed me quickly that Cho was *only* a tool, and I have to keep this in mind. But that's kind of hard at times to accept. When I think that I just can't call up Lauren, I get a bit mad.

When I see Cho's face in the paper, it really doesn't faze me anymore. The times I struggle are when I do something that I would normally do with Lauren. But then God reminds me that Lauren is in heaven right now, and hate is not something I need to be doing. You can either live your life hating people or loving people.

When I went with Lauren's dad to bring her body home, he forgave Cho right there. Lauren and her family are so on fire for God, their faith just makes them forgiving. There's no question in my mind that Lauren would have forgiven Cho, too.

The same Lauren who wrote in her journal eight months to the day before she died:

You are merciful and forgiving, personal and caring, mighty and just, omniscient and all powerful and you are MY GOD. Take control of this existence and use me.

Psychologist Dr. Julie Cox describes forgiveness as an individual process that entails complete awareness of the wrong suffered and is *not* synonymous with "It's okay that you did this."

"Forgiveness is truly giving up your right—the right that you legitimately have as a human being—to punish the offender in kind. As you do this, Jesus promises that he will give beyond what you could ask or think," Dr. Cox explains.

"For some, God will give a measure of grace and they will genuinely feel a peace and forgiveness for Cho. Yet for others, the wounds from the shootings are still very, very fresh. Grief comes in waves. Forgiveness is a process, an ebb and flow. You choose to forgive at one point, then the pain bubbles up again, and you continually give those feelings back over to God and ask him to give you his peace."

As the McCains live out their true forgiveness toward the shooter who gunned down their precious daughter, they recognize the source of their strength to make it through one day at a time, one hour at a time, one minute at a time.

"I'm not mad at the nine-millimeter and I'm not mad at a pistol. Cho was just a tool used by his master. I feel very sorry for Cho. He made eternal decisions that can never be undone," Dave McCain says. "I also feel real sorry for Cho's family. They're hurting. They lost a child just like we did.

"Nobody's offering to do things for them. They had to move because of the viciousness of people out there. Without Christ, I'm a cold vicious person, too. But Christ gives me the grace to forgive Cho because I was forgiven. God's grace is what carries us through this tragedy. And God's grace is the same as it will be a year from now, or last week, or on the day that Lauren died."

Amazing grace, how sweet in the bitterness of loss. Amazing grace, how comforting in the choice to forgive. Like the McCains, Doreen Tomlin knows full well that the sometimes arduous journey of forgiveness is lighter with God's hand to hold.

And when the Colorado Columbine flowers in the Tomlin yard poke through winter's harshness to spread into their delicate beauty, it's as if God sends a gentle reminder that the last chapter of his magnificent story does not end in death.

Perhaps this poem says it best: "Forgiveness is the fragrance of the violet which still clings fast to the heel that crushed it."

I was just reading Matt.5 w/ the B-attitudes and it ends with "Blessed are you when people persecute you for my sake" and I've not been persecuted . . . Do I speak up for you enough? I'm beginning to see opportunities where I could slip in and witness, like more than just mentioning "Hey, I'm a Christian!"

This is so vain (at least I'm consistent ☺) but I'm almost 20 and what have I done for your kingdom? How little have I yielded to you? Take my life, wherever! I'll open my mouth, but you have to loosen my tongue and speak through me! Bring me a sister, or a companion, that will hold me accountable to take the plunge in everyday life, not only in my relationship with you, but in everyday life. Do not let me waste this time you've given me! I don't know what to do, but delve into your word and make my time with you a priority! Anything else?

Open my mouth! Move my tongue to glorify you with my roommate, with my classmates, with those random people I talk to, whoever!

Show me the little things that I need to be faithful in . . .

I'm gonna have to go to bed, please wake me in the morning, with a purpose! And please give me the self discipline to run!

Lauren

[From Lauren's journal]

CHAPTER NINE

CIRCLE OF FRIENDS

*It is a great comfort to know that God is
not distant. He knows what it's like to
experience immense pain.*

—JEFF HIGHFIELD, VIRGINIA TECH CRU DIRECTOR

Phillip Zellner graduates in electrical engineering from Virginia Tech, almost four weeks after fellow senior Seung-Hui Cho made his fateful decision to not finish his college days. Cho robbed twenty-seven Hokies of their chance to receive their own diplomas. Yet May 11–12, the university bestows posthumous class rings and diplomas for these slain students in a bittersweet weekend of both celebrating the future and remembering the past.

One of twenty-year-old Phillip's closest friends and cheerleaders does not attend his commencement. Lauren McCain is not present to hug her former church youth group bud. Not present to tap on his mortarboard and joke around. Yet, in many ways, Lauren does feel present that day. Death does not keep her jubilant spirit from the hearts and minds of those who miss her most.

At times Phillip forgets that Lauren is gone. He often finds himself dialing her cell phone out of habit, and then the reality of her loss comes crashing back to him. He still can't believe that he wasn't in Norris Hall that Monday morning when parts of hell seem to bubble up on his campus. Phillip thinks back to where he was when his comrade lost her life.

I have to meet a professor at Norris that morning, but I actually wake up late. I get dressed and read the e-mail about some shooting, but I figure I'll still go to class anyway. I grab my backpack to rush over to Norris. Outside my dorm, I see cop cars and an ambulance near AJ.

I'm walking the half mile to Norris when I get to the Drillfield. I hear gunshots and see people running back across the Drillfield toward me. The police push everyone back. I'm an RA in Pritchard, so I hurry back to my dorm and get in touch with all forty-four of my guys and they are all okay.

I start to call Lauren, but I remember her phone is dead from the weekend, so I call and talk to her roommate. Later I call Lauren's parents and they are already on their way to campus.

After they arrive, I go with Lauren's dad to three hospitals looking for Lauren. Some friends and I also look for Lauren's car. We find it, which means she didn't drive from campus. We go find pictures of Lauren, so if the authorities have her body, they can identify her.

I give the pictures to the police and then just wait with Lauren's parents and a few others at the Inn. We wait in a room and pray. We just sit and wait, praying for a miracle that Lauren is alive.

I never make it to Norris Hall that day. I am within sixty feet of the building when I hear the shots. I would have been in Norris if I hadn't overslept. I never oversleep. I can't remember the last time I overslept for a class. I have three alarm clocks!

If I hadn't overslept, there's a lot better chance that I wouldn't be here today. Obviously God didn't want me to go yet. You hear stories like that all the time, but it's different when it happens to you. My parents raised me to believe that we have a big God, and now I'm seeing more of his power through all this. If it's not your time, God isn't going to let you go.

Not my time to go. I was supposed to be in that classroom. But . . .

Stories like this keep surfacing. Matt is a grader for Liviu Librescu's solid mechanics class. The VA Tech senior is supposed to be in Room 204 handing out the papers he graded over the weekend. But for the first time, Matt doesn't finish his grading—he decides to skip class instead. A solid Christian, Matt leans even harder on his faith after hearing of the carnage in Norris.

Another Christian student hurrying to Norris is hampered by foot problems. Instead of limping into his classroom, he rests in the Norris student lounge. Minutes later, the foot-sore student is locked in the lounge with other Hokies listening to the rampage unfolding above them.

Some days when CRU staff member Lisa Highfield lets memories of April 16 surface, she imagines being in Norris herself, lets her mind drift to the what-ifs.

"I wonder what it must have been like for Lauren and Mary, what were they going through," Lisa reflects. "What would I have done in the situation? What would I have seen? What if I were a college student? What if it were my sister?"

Lisa keeps a picture of Lauren in a silver-plated frame adorned with little hearts. Chum Hoang keeps a favorite picture of Lauren in a silver "Friends" frame. Chum is in the foreground with Lauren sheepishly peering over Chum's left shoulder. The girls are standing in Chum's kitchen by the fridge, the same kitchen where they wrestled up hearty cuisine for their international student friends on Friday nights.

"At our dinner discussions, Lauren would just strike up conversations so easily and comfortably. She was not afraid to invest her life in other people," Chum says, glancing over at Lauren's picture. "Lauren was not afraid to go deep in relationships. She was always asking, 'So what has God been teaching you lately? How are you doing with him?'"

It's the same Lauren who braved it out in near-freezing temperatures during a fall 2006 camping trip to Jefferson National Forest. Many of the Bridges students devour their roasted marshmallows, then drive the hour back to campus. Lauren, instead, a newbie to the international ministry, plops her sleeping bag in a large tent with several international women, some she's just met.

"Lauren had such a heart for the world," says Virginia Tech Bridges Director Blair Pippin. "We don't understand why she died now, but it helps to know Lauren would rather be in heaven than here."

The soulful Lauren would be proud of how her Virginia Tech friends, campus, and community are rethinking their priorities and widening their circle of influence since the shootings. Hit with the news of the senseless murders that Monday, the cadre of Christian ministries and churches in the rural Virginia town pull together like never before.

Within hours of the last gunshot, the Baptist Collegiate Ministries hosts an evening of reflection, worship, and prayer in their building off of Washington and Kent. An estimated 350 hurting Hokies, many of them from BCM, InterVarsity, and Campus Crusade show up in spite of their pain, in spite of them not knowing whether their missing friends are among the murdered or maimed.

Sandra Jackson, ministry representative for International Students, Inc., at Virginia Tech, comes across a number of weeping college women that night. One sits alone with her face buried in her hands, tears streaming through her fingers.

"I-I-I can't find . . . my friend . . . nobody's . . . nobody's heard from her," the young woman sobs when Sandra gently offers to help. Not far away Lauren's Bible study rejoins the CRU group, after returning from the AJ dorm without finding their friend.

The women encircle a quivering Molly, and Lisa Highfield soothingly breaks the news. "Molly, we don't know where Lauren is. Lauren had class in Norris. No one has heard from her."

The eighteen-year-old, who had awakened that morning to the first scream of the murders, collapses to the floor. Word of another dead friend smacks Molly to her knees in pure emotional exhaustion mingled with heavy tears. Molly's friends practically carry her to a nearby room where a professional counselor can help.

It reminds some of the scene in Mark 2 where four men carry their paralytic friend to a rooftop and lower him through the ceiling so the man can see Jesus. That's what close friends do for each other, especially in Blacksburg these days.

"One good thing is how the Christian community worked together in all this," says Sandra, who is back at the BCM building the next day, helping to pass out donated chips and cookies to Stone Phillips's NBC crew as they set up for filming in the building.

Yet while many Christians serve in united triage efforts, a few delve into the blame game. One Blacksburg resident tells the media, "God took the day off April sixteenth."

"This man was really angry with God and said he wasn't going to church anymore. Some others have also asked, 'Where was God that day?'" Sandra says. "Well, I turn to Psalm 115, which says, 'Not to us, O Lord, not to us, but to your name be the glory because of your love and your faithfulness. Why do the nations say, "Where is their God?" Our God is in heaven and he does whatever he pleases.' There is so much we don't understand about the shootings, but God *is* in his heaven, and he didn't take the day off even if it may *feel* like he did."

When the campus locks down the morning of April 16, Sandra e-mails and calls to check on her international student friends. Many of them are participants in her weekly English language class in the Virginia Tech student center. Sandra offers to pick up one man and drive him home from the university. Later Sandra and her husband, Pastor Bob, help support confused and grieving people gathering at Blacksburg's Montgomery Regional Hospital.

"Through this tragedy some people are examining their lives, and some are not. Some people have returned to their labs and that is where they find their solace—and life goes on," Sandra says. "I've asked my friends how this has affected them, and they just say, 'We just want to get back to normal.'"

For the Hokie nation, getting back to normal is about getting back to a *new* normal. Nothing is ordinary about a fence barricade around Norris Hall with state police on guard duty. Nothing is typical about wide maroon-and-orange ribbons tied to trees all over campus. Nothing is usual about hearing a police or an ambulance siren somewhere in Blacksburg and instantly your stomach turns queasy.

Nothing is routine about Dave and Sherry McCain missing their daughter sleeping soundly in her messy bedroom. Nothing is customary about the tears that rise up when lyrics to a song nip at the heart or another person sends sentimental condolences.

> *I have been deprived of peace; I have forgotten what*
> *prosperity is.*
> *So I say, "My splendor is gone and all that I had hoped*
> *from the Lord."*
> *I remember my affliction and my wandering, the bit-*
> *terness and the gall.*
> *I well remember them, and my soul is downcast*
> *within me.*
> *Yet this I call to mind and therefore I have hope:*
> *Because of the Lord's great love we are not consumed,*
> *for his compassions never fail.*
> *They are new every morning; great is your faith-*
> *fulness.*
>
> —LAMENTATIONS 3:17–23 (NIV)

"God's mercies 'are new every morning.' I knew this in my head from the Scripture in Lamentations 3 and the chorus to 'Great Is Thy Faithfulness,' but now I've lived this. God is writing his new mercies on my heart with each new day," Sherry explains. "I now know what it's like to have others carry my burdens. It is also reassuring to know that if we didn't love so deeply, we wouldn't feel loss so deeply."

Nationwide, thousands of people from elementary students in Alaska to VFW groups in Florida, to churches in Texas and scout troops in the Northeast, send their condolences and words of support to Virginia Tech. Hundreds of banners, cards, posters, and handmade craft items—in a bright array of colors, with countless personal messages and signatures—line the halls and the ballroom of the Virginia Tech student center. One memorial submission is a photograph of a green plant sprouting out of an empty gun-shell casing, a symbol of new life emerging from death.

"We're thinking of you and praying for you."

"Our hearts hurt with yours."

"You will prevail. Go Hokies."

There is strength and solace in the handwritten messages, e-mailed prayers, and the loving bonds of community—something the loner Cho missed out on for much of his life. And with his malicious intent to harm and destroy, perhaps the killer underestimates the resolve of the tens of thousands of others left behind to counter his vengeance with caring and camaraderie.

With the campus on summer break, Virginia Tech CRU Director Jeff Highfield sits at Mill Mountain Coffee & Tea, his regular hangout just across from campus on North Main. Mill Mountain's watercolor painting of Prince Edward Island against the deep apricot walls looks so serene in contrast to this rural Virginia town's recent upheaval. Beaches versus bullets. Some things in life just never make sense.

Jeff sips his java and reflects on the mind-boggling loss and recovery etched deeply into the minds and hearts of the more than five hundred students under his helm. Last fall, as the new CRU director, Jeff led the group through a monthlong series on building community. He never imagined how intensely his staff and students would need to apply his words in mid-April.

"The biggest thing that helped us get through was to be in community—just being with people that care about you, that you care about," says Jeff. "On the surface most of us are pretty set with our needs met. This tragedy forced us to be real, to be dependent on each other."

Jeff talks about the new depths of their relationships. Friends who cry in public or ask for prayer. Friends who go beyond social niceness to transparent honesty. Friends all touched by death's vicious sting.

"The Bible talks about Jesus as the suffering servant, a man of sorrows, and acquainted with grief. He knows exactly what we are going through," Jeff says. "It is a great comfort to know that God is not distant. He knows what it's like to experience immense pain.

"Through our grief and pain we feel like a really tight-knit family now. I think the transparency and authenticity will continue this fall and beyond. Community is a key to seeing this generation come to know the Lord, as young people are not just hearing about the gospel, but seeing the gospel lived out in authentic community among their peers."

The kind of community Lauren thrived in: the huddling with sleeping bags on a frosty fall night, the serving chili and cornbread to famished guests from abroad. The joining together for the last CRU meeting of the year, where some six hundred mourning regulars and visitors alike lift their voices in prayer and song. The honoring of graduating seniors and the honoring of Jarrett, Mary, and Lauren, who've already graduated to heaven.

Man, can you believe I'm 20? ¼ of my life is gone! It's quite an eye opener. Take this life, I can't focus on what I want in college or those desires to be popular—or completely me—pleasure oriented. There's not time!

Psalm 66:10–12
For you, O God, tested us;
You refined us like silver.
You let men ride over our heads;
We went through fire and water,
But you brought us to a place of abundance.

This past year has felt like fire and water. I escaped from one place to fall into a more emotionally painful one.

But through it you have broken me of a sin I thought was impossible to be free from. And in fulfilling my "dreams" I know the only thing I will be satisfied with is you. The only thing that brings my heart true joy and peace is you. I've run after things, thoughts and ambitions, and I know they're empty. Only in you can I find my purpose. What a wonderful thing!

Show me your purpose for me at Tech. and on this earth. But, if you choose not to, I will still praise you and walk where you lead, not because I am selfless, or holy, or "determined to sacrifice myself to do what is right" but because you are the delight of my heart and I cannot live without you. You are what makes my dreams pleasant. Whether I work in an orphanage in Russia, or be a housewife with 1 child, if you are not my purpose, if you aren't the one orchestrating it all, it's not worth it

How awesome are your deeds,
So great is your power that
Your enemies cringe before you,
All the earth bows down to you;
They sing praise to you,
They sing praise to your name.

♥

[From Lauren's journal]

CHAPTER TEN

DANCING
BEFORE HIM

*Your impact on so many lives, including my
own, is astounding. You really loved God
and now you can finally dance before Him.
I love you, Lauren.*

—CASEY!, MYSPACE.COM, APRIL 17, 2007

In the days following the massacre at Virginia's largest university, one might envision the surrounding Blue Ridge Mountains a deeper, somber blue, almost as if the meandering hills are in mourning themselves. As the dreary clouds of despair begin to part over Blacksburg, hordes of students gather at The Cellar or Rivermill. They meet for pizza at Backstreets, or at Poor Billy's for sushi.

Local folks sit in the roomy wooden booths at Our Daily Bread, exchanging the latest *Roanoke Times* news about the tragedy between bites of fresh baked lemon-poppyseed bread and ricotta cheesecake.

Amid all the banter and occasional stress-relieving laughter, the conversations include a smattering of fear, worry, and anger. As one woman eating a late lunch at Our Daily Bread summarizes, "These emotions are really indications of deeper spiritual matters."

And from her brick rental house with the white picket fence, Chum Hoang thinks back to Friday afternoon, April 13, with her disciple Lauren McCain. This afternoon the two friends split a decadent piece of Mississippi chocolate pie at Deet's Place in celebration of Chum's twenty-first birthday the day before. Treasured friends enjoying rich chocolate and rich conversation. Young college women with the whole world ahead of them. Does it get any better than this?

Savoring the last slivers of their dessert, Chum and Lauren recite the verses to Colossians 1, just the beginning of their quest to memorize the entire book written from a first-century Roman prison.

We give thanks to God, the Father of our Lord Jesus Christ, praying always for you, since we heard of your faith in Christ Jesus and the love which you have for all the saints; because of the hope laid up for you in heaven, of which you previously heard in the word of truth, the gospel, which has come to you, just as in all the world also it is constantly bearing fruit and increasing, even as it has been doing in you also since

the day you heard of it and understood the grace of
God in truth . . .

—COLOSSIANS 1:3–6 (NASB)

"We got really excited about words 'the hope laid up in heaven' and how God has 'qualified us to share in the inheritance of the saints,' " Chum recalls with a smile. "A week or so before, we started talking about heaven and Lauren remarked, 'I'm so excited about heaven. I'm ready to go.' "

Little did Chum know that some sixty hours later, her dear friend would be in heaven. Little did Chum know that her recent devotions about broken hearts and Jesus saying, 'Come to me and give me your burdens,' would hit so close to home starting that blustery Monday.

For this reason also, since the day we heard of it, we
have not ceased to pray for you and to ask that you
may be filled with the knowledge of his will in all
spiritual wisdom and understanding.

—COLOSSIANS 1:9 (NASB)

Molly Donohue thinks back to the last time she saw Lauren. Their Bible study met in West AJ the Wednesday night before the shootings. All of the young women recall noticing something about the way Lauren read aloud when it was her turn to read from her Bible.

"She read her passage with just so much passion and energy that I think Dana even made her read it again," Molly says. "We all just commented on how Lauren took something such as reading a Bible passage to a whole other level."

According to her family and friends, Lauren took most of her life to a whole other level. McCain family friend Karen Macri taught history and literature in Lauren's homeschool co-op. "You just never met anyone like Lauren. She wanted to know the ins and outs of everything. You'd better be ready to defend your position when you were talking to her," Karen says with a fond chuckle. "Lauren was never disrespectful, though. And when she was talking to you, you felt like you were the only one there."

The twenty-year-old's intense interest in other people certainly caught the attention of her peers. "At CRU, I remember seeing Lauren talking to people who don't necessarily get the time of day from most people, you know? The people who are kind of on the outskirts," Julie Harrison comments. "I always noticed that Lauren was talking to them, and she inspired me to reach out to people, and not just because of people's status or popularity. Lauren was just accepting of a lot of different kinds of people.

She was totally the same with everyone—really genuine."

Lauren's CRU friends find themselves saying, "You didn't have to be best friends with Lauren to be best friends with Lauren." Lauren's passion for relationships is one reason why more than a thousand people attended her funeral in Hampton, Virginia, on Sunday, April 22.

Pastor Leonard Riley from her home church, Restoration Church—Phoebus Baptist, reads from Matthew 5:13–16 and challenges the audience to be "salt and light" to the world like Lauren. He ends his message with a call for people to examine their own relationships with God, their own eternal destiny. Twenty-eight-year-old R. J. Deel is one of a handful of people who walks forward in an expression of faith.

I didn't know Lauren personally. I looked on the news and saw where the funeral was going to be. I felt I needed to be there. The tragedy really touched me. I think her death affected a lot of people.

I looked at Lauren's MySpace page and so many others seem so negative. Not hers. That's her own personal memorial that she created for herself. She pretty much walked like Jesus walked.

As soon as I pulled into the church parking lot, I could tell a spiritual presence was there, not a sadness, but a happy sort of sad. I heard her family and friends say how she made an impact on everybody. I felt like I needed to do the same thing. It's been so long since I shed a tear.

I made my own commitment to Jesus back in 2001 but slid in my faith. I knew I needed to rededicate myself, but I'd been putting that off and putting that off. But you never know what tomorrow holds. You never know what the next hour holds.

I wanted to dedicate myself because I want to go to heaven. I want to do something with my life. I want to make a change. I don't want a day to go by when I'm not making some sort of difference in somebody's life. Like Lauren, I want to be remembered for good when I die.

Lauren Ashley McCain is remembered for good and her faith in a good God. "I left the funeral and I felt more encouraged and more strengthened than when I had walked in the church," says Dana Cox, who rode with her Bible-study women the 225 miles to the service. "After the funeral, Lauren's mom said something that will stay with me for a very long time. She said, 'Lauren is doing what she's always wanted to do—praising her Father in heaven.

And no matter how much I miss her, I would never ask her to come back.'"

For He delivered us from the domain of darkness, and transferred us to the kingdom of His beloved Son, in whom we have redemption, the forgiveness of sins.

—COLOSSIANS 1:13–14 (NASB)

Although Lauren and the thirty-one others killed at Virginia Tech are not coming back, and Lauren's friends miss their vivacious pal, they are more determined than ever to make their Creator known at the university. The CRU gobbletalk.com website posts the "Where Is God in the Midst of Tragedy?" article (see appendix) and receives almost eleven thousand hits the first two weeks after the shootings. This website normally receives an average of six hundred visitors a month. Of the nearly eleven thousand visitors, sixty-six expressed an interest in knowing Christ personally.

The Virginia Tech CRU staff see these positive spiritual inquiries and decisions as part of the legacy of the slain Christians on their campus. Lauren McCain's closest Hokie friends are not about to let their comrade's life pass in vain.

"After talking to my friends, we realize that Lauren's legacy has inspired us to live a life worthy of Christ—she *lived* that life and she ran the race and now she's finished. But we're still here, and we can do something about it," Julie Harrison explains. "We can do more than just say, 'Oh, Lauren was such a great girl.' We can *actually* live full out for God.

"I feel like our campus before April 16 was somewhat spiritually apathetic. But I think now people are understanding there's a difference between good and evil, and they see that what Cho did was evil. People are now definitely questioning where they go after they die. We all need to know God and the time is now, not next week. It's now."

Someone who now understands the cruel difference between good and evil is a student who was shot multiple times by Cho—and lived. Days after he is released from the hospital, the young man turns to a local Blacksburg pastor and asks how to find peace with God. Now when the survivor looks at his scars from the shooting, he is reminded how close he came to death and is grateful that he never needs to fear death again.

And Molly, who encountered death on the other side of her bedroom wall, still sometimes hears the terrifying shrieks of her friend—the sounds that first alert the world to America's most notorious mass murderer. Yet, moving forward, Molly chooses to focus on the fun memories of her departed friends.

Molly finds great comfort in remembering the night her "directionally challenged" Bible-study bud, Lauren, led her and another friend on a roundabout trip to Wal-Mart. Confused and lost, the three collegians eventually find the store and return late to the campus parking lot.

With the night air briskly turning their cheeks a numb pink, and the other two freshmen grumbling about the chilly, long walk back to their dorm, Lauren suddenly turns to her girlfriends. She leans her head back and almost shouts, "Look at that moon!"

"Lauren starts talking about how she's awed that people don't believe in God when there's such beauty in creation like this," Molly recalls, pausing to soak in the fond remembrance. "So I sort of roll my eyes and say, 'Lauren, you would say that.'"

With a broad beam of contentment on her rosy face, Lauren glances at her two shivering friends—then focuses her delighted eyes back on the moon.

And when Dave and Sherry McCain think of their exuberant daughter, they lift their eyes heavenward. "Satan took his best shot. He didn't get any glory out of this,"

Sherry explains. "Lauren gained. We lost. We lost her, but she didn't lose anything. She gained everything. She has her reward."

Sherry pauses. Through gentle tears she ponders the bittersweet mingling of joy and sorrow that wells in her heart. "I can just see Lauren in heaven, see her dancing before God, touching his face, and saying, 'Wow, look how beautiful he is.' When you think about it, it's reassuring. . . . Our days on Earth, they're just a blink of an eye compared to eternity."

In times when the windows were painted black, my God was there and the "radar" led me into all truth, though I didn't know it then. God's plan in leading me the way He did was so different from what I thought it was. So when things didn't work out as I thought they should I assumed God had left me (ha) or I was in sin the whole time and unable to hear Him. Now, however, I think I know why He allowed that and He's confirming it in my life now. I'm amazed how much He's growing my character while still taking care of me. It almost makes me want to go through the valley again (almost . . .)

But He spoke to me the whole time, through His word, I wrote it down. When my mind was too muddled and torn and my spirit was paralyzed, he still spoke to me and I could be sure it was Him, b/c it was supported (and based upon) His word.

[Notes from Lauren's Bible study, undated]

A LETTER FROM
SHERRY McCAIN

"The worst scenario for us would be the best thing for Lauren." As my husband said those words, I knew he was right. We knew something was terribly wrong, and as we headed to Virginia Tech we just kept praying for a miracle.

Lauren wasn't the type of girl to allow anyone to worry. That no one had heard from her was hard evidence of the severity of the situation. We were hoping she was just injured and we hadn't been notified yet, but as the seconds ticked by, the reality of our worst nightmare descended like a fog. In the mind-numbing silence we reached for God's Word, a lifeline and a comfort.

I read from the Psalms. "He who dwells in the secret place of the Most High shall abide under the shadow of the Almighty. I will say of the Lord, 'He is my refuge and my fortress; My God, in Him I will trust'" (Psalm 91:1–2, NKJV).

We knew Lauren's heart. She loved the Lord with all that she was. To see her worship or hear her pray was to see her before her God. Her passion for him was evident in her words and actions and we knew without a doubt that in his presence was where she would want to be above anything else.

While en route, we heard that her body was not at the morgue and we felt some hope. She was also not listed among the wounded and we called all the hospitals again hoping she was at one of them. When we finally reached the Inn at VT we found out that all the victims had not been moved from the scene and the waiting continued. One very kind State Police Officer kept looking at me with such compassion and I wanted to say, "Yes, I know that you've seen her."

God allowed us time before finding out about Lauren so that we weren't completely overwhelmed, and all through the night and next day we kept praying for a miracle. We knew that our God is big and not bound in the least by circumstances. He could provide regardless of the hopelessness of the situation. We kept asking.

God put eight precious people with us to walk though the darkness: Tim Porter, a pastor we met within minutes of our arrival: our pastor, Leonard Riley; a friend and deacon, Rob Hall; friends Steve and Helen Parke; Jessica Hawkins, Lauren's roommate; Ruth Castillo, her close friend; and Phillip Zellner, Lauren's close friend from home and college. They prayed for and with us, cared for us when we couldn't think, and waited with us. We were never alone. God was with us in his Spirit and in his children that he placed around us. Every person we encountered from the college, the Blacksburg police, and the Virginia State Police was kind, patient, and compassionate.

In the days that followed, as we made arrangements for Lauren's funeral, God placed people all around who took care of us and walked with us through this enormously difficult time. The smallest detail was not overlooked. He provided people to pray for us all around the world. Everywhere we looked we saw blessing upon blessing. "But you are a shield around me, O Lord; you bestow glory on me and lift up my head" (Psalm 3:3, NIV).

As we learned the details of Lauren's death, I realized that God had granted a prayer from long ago.

I had a fear of losing one of my children early. I dedicated them each to God as soon as I knew I was pregnant and acknowledged that they were his and he was their protector. As I felt afraid I spoke to God and asked him that if he did take one of them home early that it be quick so they would not be hurt or afraid. We found out from one of the survivors that Lauren's class was laughing just before the shooter came in and shot the professor. Lauren was probably shot right after that. We know that she died instantly and we believe she didn't have time to realize what was happening. This was surely God's provision.

God's blessings have been so great in everything that happened we have only one thing to mourn— that Lauren isn't with us. We miss her so much, but we don't mourn for Lauren because she is with Jesus. She has lost nothing compared to what she has gained and we wouldn't bring her back. We only mourn our loss. And in our mourning he still comforts us. Even in that we don't mourn as those "who have no hope" (1 Thesalonians 4:13, NIV), I know I will see her again as surely as I know I'll see my Lord.

*Lauren's life song was Psalm 37:3–4 (NKJV),
"Trust in the Lord, and do good; dwell in the land,
and feed on His faithfulness. Delight yourself also in
the Lord, and He shall give you the desires of your
heart." Lauren's desire was to minister to the international community as well as to every person she
met with the love of Jesus and the truth that he is the
Son of God and the Savior of the world. Lauren's
testimony of Jesus Christ being the love of her life
has been quoted by newspapers and magazines all
over the world. God is granting the desire of her
heart to a magnitude she could never have imagined.
What a great and mighty God!*

*Lauren was unique. She had a quirky sense of
humor and was the zest in our life. We feel quite flat
without her. She was such a presence, a delight, and a
joy. Every minute her absence is keenly evident, but so
is the fact that she was an amazing blessing and true
gift from God to us. We still cry and cry out to God for
comfort and peace. He always hears and fills us. He is
never absent as he was never absent from Lauren. He
walked with her every day and all the way home and
he will walk with us all the way as well. "I lift up my
eyes to the hills—where does my help come from? My*

help comes from the Lord, the Maker of heaven and earth" (Psalm 121:1–2, NIV).

> *In Christ's Love,*
> *Sherry McCain*
> *(Lauren's mother)*

IN MEMORIAM

Ross Abdallah Alameddine, 20, Saugus, Massachusetts, sophomore English major, with minors in French and business. Ross was a graduate of Austin Preparatory School in Reading, Massachusetts, where he played piano and sang at the school's coffeehouse. He was also active in French and Debate clubs at Austin. A music fanatic who loved jazz, Ross excelled as a video-game enthusiast and computer whiz.

Christopher James "Jamie" Bishop, 35, Blacksburg, Virginia, instructor in Foreign Languages and Literature (German). Although his courses were legendarily rigorous, "Herr Bishop" was popular with his students and readily offered individual attention to help them succeed. Jamie earned his bachelor and master's degrees at the University of Georgia, and as a Fulbright Scholar studied at the Christian-Albrechts-Universität in Kiel, Germany. At Virginia Tech, Jamie also taught classes via the Faculty Development Institute. Jamie is survived by his wife, Stefanie Hofer.

Brian Roy Bluhm, 25, Cedar Rapids, Iowa, civil-engineering grad student. A teaching assistant, Brian received his undergraduate degree from Virginia Tech and was preparing to defend his master's thesis. Brian was a member of the V-Tech Alumni Association, American Society of Civil Engineers, and the Baptist Collegiate Ministries. He exemplified his love for Christ through his kindness and memorable laugh. Brian was passionate about Detriot Tigers baseball and Virginia Tech sports, especially football and basketball.

Ryan Christopher "Stack" Clark, 22, Martinez, Georgia, a fifth-year student working toward a triple-degree in psychology, biology, and English, while carrying a 4.0 grade-point average. A distinguished campus leader, Ryan played the baritone in the Marching Virginians university band and served as musical director at Camp Big Heart. A resident advisor in West Ambler Johnston Hall, Ryan planned to pursue a doctorate in neuroscience and work with the mentally impaired.

Austin Michelle Cloyd, 19, Blacksburg, Virginia, sophomore international studies and French major. Austin enjoyed world travel with her family and politics, as well as international and environmental issues. Austin loved children and served as day-camp counselor for Fellowship of Christian Athletes, a group leader for the Champaign-Urbana Service Project, and a swimming instructor at the Virginia Tech McComas Hall. A basketball player herself, Austin relished college basketball games, reading, music concerts, and scuba diving.

Jocelyne Couture-Nowak, 49, Blacksburg, Virginia, French language teacher. Jocelyne, who was born in Montreal, Canada, and helped create the École Acadienne de Truro, the first French school in Nova Scotia. Jocelyne's *joie de vivre* is well remembered by her family, friends, students, and colleagues. Her graceful energy overflowed in her love of nature and in the preservation of her francophone heritage. Jocelyne is survived by her husband, Jerzy Nowak, who teaches horticulture at Virgina Tech, and two daughters.

Kevin P. Granata, 45, Blacksburg, Virginia, professor in the Department of Engineering Science and Mechanics. Kevin served in the military and conducted orthopedic research in hospitals before going to Virginia Tech, where he was considered one of the top five biomechanics researchers in the country, specializing in cerebral palsy movement dynamics. At Virginia Tech he established and co-directed the Musculoskeletal Biomechanics Laboratory. Kevin is survived by his wife, Linda, and their children, Eric, Alex, and Ellen.

Matthew Gregory Gwaltney, 24, Chester, Virginia, graduate student in civil and environmental engineering. Matthew was a second-year master's student in the Charles E. Via Department of Civil and Environmental Engineering. A magna cum laude Virginia Tech graduate in 2005, and member of several national honor societies, Matthew's graduate work included teaching civil engineering labs and conducting research on storm water management. Named as "best guy to take home to your parents" in high school, Matthew enjoyed working on river mechanics and river restoration projects, but also left time to play basketball and baseball with his friends.

Caitlin Millar Hammaren, 19, Westtown, New York, sophomore international studies and French major with a minor in leadership and social change. A member of Kappa Kappa Gamma and a dorm resident advisor, Caitlin devoted great care to her residents. Her leadership efforts were awarded with an induction into the National Residence

Hall Honorary, an organization that recognizes the top one percent of residence hall leaders. Caitlin dedicated her time outside her studies to many activities including riding horses, singing, and playing violin.

Jeremy Michael Herbstritt, 27, Bellefonte, Pennsylvania, graduate student in the Department of Civil and Environmental Engineering. Jeremy earned three undergraduate degrees from Penn State in biochemistry, molecular biology, and civil engineering. At Virginia Tech, Jeremy served as a teaching assistant for the Fluid Mechanics for Civil and Environmental Engineers class. Jeremy was awarded the Sussman Scholarship for summer 2007 and planned to conduct research on the Lower Roanoke River in North Carolina as part of the project and his thesis. Jeremy loved to hike, kayak, bike, ski, and work on the family farm.

Rachael Elizabeth Hill, 18, Glen Allen, Virginia, freshman in biology. Rachael planned to earn a Ph.D. in biochemistry, specializing in nanotechnology. She graduated from Grove Avenue Christian School, where she was the star of her high school volleyball team. An accomplished classical pianist, Rachael had studied piano since she was six years old. She loved to read—especially novels and the Bible—and enjoyed classic movies, playing volleyball, and time with family and friends. A dedicated follower of Jesus Christ, Rachael's personal goal was to honor God in everything.

Emily Jane Hilscher, 19, Woodville, Virginia, freshman animal and poultry sciences major. Emily was said to glow in her love of life, animals, friends and family, and cooking. She intended to complete an eight-year journey at Virginia Tech culminating in her becoming a veterinarian at an equine practice. Emily was a skilled horsewoman, became a member of the Virginia Tech equestrian team in spring 2007, and was a member of the Intercollegiate Horse Shows Association.

Jarrett Lee Lane, 22, Narrows, Virginia, senior civil engineering major. Jarrett excelled both in sports and academics throughout his life. Earning honors as class valedictorian in high school, Jarrett also became the school's top tennis team player and earned all-district honors in football, basketball, and track. At Virginia Tech Jarrett played intramural sports and became a member of the university's Campus Crusade for Christ group. As a senior, Jarrett was awarded The Stanley and Frances Cohen Scholarship, a civil engineering scholarship. One to focus on living life to the fullest, Jarrett left behind a rich legacy of deep relationships with family and friends.

Matthew Joseph La Porte, 20, Dumont, New Jersey, sophomore in political science attending Virginia Tech on an Air Force ROTC scholarship. Matt was preparing for a commission in the United States Air Force, with the goal to be an active duty intelligence officer. As a member of the Virginia Tech corps of cadets, Matthew enjoyed playing tenor drum for the Regimental Band, the Highty-Tighties. He was also a selected member of the school's cadet jazz band.

Henry J. Lee (Henh Ly), 20, Roanoke, Virginia, sophomore in computer engineering. The ninth of ten children, Henry moved with his family from Vietnam to Roanoke, Virginia, in 1994. An academic achiever, Henry graduated as his high school class salutatorian with a 4.47 grade point average and was already on the dean's list at Virginia Tech. He displayed another side to his keen mind with his creativity through origami and photography. Fond of watching movies and hanging out with his friends, Henry proudly became an American citizen in May 2006.

Liviu Librescu, 76, Blacksburg, Virginia, Department of Engineering Science and Mechanics professor. Growing up in Romania during World War II, Liviu survived the Holocaust to pursue a distinguished career in aeronautical engineering. Liviu earned his doctorate at the Academy of

Science of Romania and taught seven years at Tel-Aviv University before accepting a full-time position at Virginia Tech in 1985. The renowned aeronautical engineering educator and researcher is survived by his wife, Marlena, and his sons, Joseph and Arieh, who reside in Israel. Liviu was posthumously awarded the Grand Cross of Romania, the nation's highest civilian honor.

G. V. Loganathan, 53, Blacksburg, Virginia, civil and environmental engineering professor. Born in Tamil Nadu, India, G. V. earned a Ph.D. in civil engineering at Purdue University and joined the Virginia Tech faculty in December 1981. G. V. became one of the university's most respected educators and earned numerous teaching honors. One of America's top researchers in hydrology and water resources systems, municipal water supply professionals have relied extensively on his findings. G. V. directly supervised about fifty Ph.D. and master's degree students at Virginia Tech. Married to Usha, with two daughters, Uma and Abhi, G. V. won the university's prestigious 2006 Wine Award for Excellence in Teaching.

Partahi Mamora "Mora" Halomoan Lombantoruan, 35, Blacksburg, Virginia, Ph.D. student in civil engineering. Mora earned his B.S. and master's degrees in civil engineering in his native Indonesia before arriving in Blacksburg in 2004. Known for his contagious smile and patient, compassionate personality, Mora reveled in Virginia Tech and became a true Hokies football fan. The international street fair will not be the same without his grilled saté. Somewhat shy and soft-spoken, Mora was quick to join lively political, intellectual, and spiritual discussions. His many friends and Hokie peers will miss his wise and serving spirit.

Lauren Ashley McCain, 20, Hampton, Virginia, freshman in international studies. Lauren described her Virginia Tech experience as "almost heaven." Striving for excellence in her studies, Lauren often spoke to her professors and teaching assistants and never settled for less than her best. Her quirky sense of humor, love of life, and caring heart blessed many friends and peers. Active in many groups on campus, Lauren also fully enjoyed playing intramural soccer and women's flag football. She had a long-standing love of the German language and culture. Because of Lauren's love of Jesus Christ, she was active in Campus Crusade for Christ, New Life Christian Fellowship, and Bridges International Ministries.

Daniel Patrick O'Neil, 22, Lincoln, Rhode Island, environmental engineering graduate student and teaching assistant. Daniel earned his B.S. in civil engineering at Lafayette College in Easton, Pennsylvania, where he was an EXCEL Scholar. Daniel traveled to most Western European countries and lived a semester in Brussels, Belgium. After graduation, he planned to live in Dublin, Ireland. An avid Hokie football and basketball fan, Daniel enjoyed many outdoor activities including running, biking, skateboarding, and backpacking. Daniel excelled at writing and playing music and his friends plan to make a CD of his signature music.

Juan Ramón Ortiz-Ortiz, 26, Bayamon, Puerto Rico, graduate student in engineering. Juan earned a bachelor's degree in civil engineering at the Polytechnic University of Puerto Rico, where he was chapter president of the American Society of Civil Engineering and a member of numerous professional organizations. In August 2006, Juan and his wife, Liselle, started together in Virginia Tech's master's program in civil engineering. He planned a teaching career. Fond of salsa dancing, Juan played timbales in a family band and for a college choir. He lived life with a love for God and participated in several Catholic activities as a youth. Juan is dearly remembered for his dedicated and patient demeanor and radiant smile.

Minal Hiralal Panchal, 26, Mumbai, India, graduate architecture student concentrating on advanced building structures and energy-efficient designs. In India, Minal, known as "Minu" to her family, excelled in the state-level architecture entrance test and in her senior design solution at Rizvi College of Architecture. She enrolled in the master's program at Virginia Tech in August 2006 and worked for the Virginia Tech STARS (Summer Training Academy for Rising Students) program. Minal desired to be a respected architect like her father. A watercolor painter, poet, and swimmer, Minal was blessed with childlike enthusiasm and is remembered as the bright, caring girl who helped the neighborhood children with their schoolwork.

Daniel Alejandro Perez, 21, Woodbridge, Virginia, and Peru, junior in international studies. Daniel moved from his native Peru with his mother and sister in 2000. An accomplished athlete in high school, Daniel graduated with honors in 2004. He attended two community colleges before enrolling at Virginia Tech in fall 2006. Nicknamed "Korki" because of his unexpected, goofy side, Daniel loved to make his friends and family happy. A hard worker, Daniel pursued an international services career as a means to draw people together and bring peaceful harmony to the world.

Erin Nicole Peterson, 18, Chantilly, Virginia, freshman international studies major. Erin's parents considered their only child an "angel—their dewdrop from heaven." In high school Erin was a member of the National Honor Society and a skilled basketball player, leading her team as captain her senior year. Grounded with a sure moral compass, Erin lived life joyfully and her magnetic spirit blessed all her knew her. Erin loved spending time with her family and faithfully believed in the power of prayer. Not long before her death, Erin was elected co-president of EMPOWER, an organization that builds self-esteem and confidence in young minority girls.

Michael Steven Pohle, Jr., 23, Flemington, New Jersey, senior biological sciences major. An avid adventurer and overcomer, Mike used his childhood teasing over speech development issues to shape his preserving spirit. Earning his black belt in karate, Mike also enjoyed playing a variety of sports including soccer, lacrosse, and football. At Virginia Tech Mike played midfield on the men's lacrosse team for two years. In his honor, the team wore his initials on their helmets in a conference tournament shortly after his death. Mike excelled in science and his instructors considered him a model student. Sensitive to the challenges of others, Mike befriended many an underdog—helping others was part of his giving spirit.

Julia Kathleen Pryde, age 23, Middletown, New Jersey, graduate student in biological systems engineering. A dedicated environmentalist, Julia traveled in summer 2006 to Ecuador and Peru to research water quality issues and assist poor Andes residents with sustainable agriculture methods. A certified wild-land firefighter, Julia deployed as part of a firefighting team to help fight the 2005 Arizona fires. Always in pursuit of bettering the world and herself, Julia reflected a warm, generous, accepting spirit that embraced diverse people and broad societal challenges. Julia planned to pursue a doctorate and teach at the college level focusing on pure water and sustainable agriculture efforts in Africa and the Andes.

Mary Karen Read, 19, Annandale, Virginia, freshman in interdisciplinary studies. Born at the U.S. Army hospital in Seoul, South Korea, Mary lived with her family in several U.S. states before they settled in Virginia. In high school Mary played lacrosse for two years and was a member of the National Honor Society, the Tri-M Band Honor Society, and the French Honor Society. A clarinet section leader, Mary was also president of the Annandale High

School band. Mary loved children, especially her five younger siblings, and was considering an elementary education career. Passionate about her faith, Mary was a member of Campus Crusade for Christ at Virginia Tech and applied to be a Bible-study leader for the group. On April 16 she would have learned of her acceptance as a Bible-study leader starting in the fall.

Reema Joseph Samaha, 18, Centreville, Virginia, freshman in French and international studies. Embracing her Lebanese heritage, Reema was an active member of the Melkite Greek Catholic Church and traveled to the Middle East studying the languages and cultures. She shared her family's soccer passion and was named to three youth soccer all-star teams. Creative and witty, Reema was also an avid dancer and actor, performing with Virginia Tech's Contemporary Dance Ensemble and the Hill and Veil Middle Eastern Dance Group. A summa cum laude graduate of Westfield High, Reema received awards for her performances, including one as featured dancer in *Fiddler on the Roof.* Pursuing a major in urban planning, Reema earned a 4.0 grade point at Virginia Tech.

Waleed Mohamed Shaalan, 32, Zagazig, Egypt, doctoral student in civil engineering. Beginning his Ph.D. program in Egypt, Waleed transferred to Virginia Tech in fall 2006 after the university offered him an assistantship. Like his father, Waleed was dedicated and passionate about civil engineering. An active participant in the Muslim Student Association at Virginia Tech, Waleed enjoyed being a part of the group's community activities. In spite of his rigorous schedule, Waleed reached out to the people around him and was known for his wide smile and friendly wave. Waleed is survived by his wife, Amira, and young son, Khaled, who were planning soon to move from Egypt to Blacksburg.

Leslie Geraldine Sherman, 20, Springfield, Virginia, junior in history and international studies. Passionate about history and an avid world traveler, Leslie was headed to Russia for a six-week summer program. She previously saved her own money for two trips to Argentina and Ecuador, which fueled her passion for exploration. Outside of her academic achievements, Leslie often gave of her herself as a retirement home student volunteer, tutor, and a Special Olympics coach. A marathon runner, Leslie displayed incredible strength and courage. She planned to graduate and serve the less fortunate through the Peace Corps, then pursue a U.S. State Department career.

Maxine "Max" Shelly Turner, 22, Vienna, Virginia, senior chemical engineering major. "Max" to her friends and family, the exceptional honors student excelled in schoolwork and many additional arenas including swing dancing, Tae Kwon Do, and violin. Max reveled in the video game *The Legend of Zelda* and made all her accomplishments look easy. At Virginia Tech she helped found a chapter of Alpha Omega Epsilon, a sorority for women in engineering, and was an active member and officer in the chapter. Max also volunteered in the college and community through the Big Event, Relay for Life, and the local animal shelter.

Nicole Regina White, 20, Smithfield, Virginia, junior international studies major with a minor in political science. A generous giver of her time and energy, Nicole completed emergency medical training in high school and served with her community's Volunteer Rescue Squad. A YMCA lifeguard and swimming instructor in her hometown, Nicole continued her volunteering efforts in Blacksburg through her work with the local battered women's shelter and animal shelter. Nicole accepted people for more than their outward appearance and, through her home church outreach program, helped take the message of Christ's love and forgiveness to others.

WHERE IS GOD
IN THE MIDST OF TRAGEDY?

Where can we find inner strength to cope with
fears, tragedy, disaster, and terrorist attacks?
What exactly can we count on God for?

To what degree can we rely on God to be with us? Is he really someone we can turn to at all . . . in times of crisis as well as times of calm?

Tragedy, Disaster, Terrorist Attacks: Where Is God?

God is the Creator of the universe who yearns for us to know him. That is why we are all here. It is his desire that we rely on and experience his strength, love, justice, holiness, and compassion. So he says to all who are willing, "Come to me."

Unlike us, God knows what will happen tomorrow, next week, next year, the next decade. He says, "I am God, and there is no one like Me, declaring the end from the beginning."[1] He knows what will happen in the world. More importantly, He knows what will occur in your life and can be there for you, if you've chosen to include him in your life. He tells us that he can be "our refuge and strength, an ever-present help in trouble."[2] But we must make a sincere effort to seek him. He says, "You will seek Me and find Me, when you search for Me with all your heart."[3]

That doesn't mean that those who know God will escape difficult times. They won't. When castastrophic suffering and death strike, those who know God will be involved in that suffering also. But there is a peace and a strength that God's presence gives. One follower of Jesus Christ put it this way: "We are hard pressed on every side, but not crushed; perplexed, but not in despair; persecuted, but not abandoned; struck down, but not destroyed."[4] Reality tells us that we will experience problems in life. However, if we go through them while knowing God, we can react to them with a different perspective and with a strength that is not our own. No problem has the capacity to be insurmountable to God. He is bigger than all the problems that can hit us, and we are not left alone to deal with them.

God's Word tells us, "The Lord is good, a refuge in times of trouble. He cares for those who trust in him."[5] And, "The Lord is near to all who call on him, to all who call on him in truth. He fulfills the desires of those who fear him; he hears their cry and saves them."[6]

Jesus Christ told his followers these comforting words: "Are not two sparrows sold for a cent? And yet not one of them will fall to the ground apart from your Father. But the very hairs of your head are all numbered. So do not fear; you are more valuable than many sparrows."[7] If you truly turn to God, he will care for you as no one else does, and in a way that no one else can.

Tragedy, Disaster, Terrorist Attacks: Our Free Will

God has created humanity with the ability to choose. This means that we are not forced into a relationship with him. He allows us to reject him and to commit other evil acts as well. He could force us to be loving. He could force us to be good. But then what kind of relationship would we have with him? It would not be a relationship at all, but a forced, absolutely controlled obedience. Instead he gave us the human dignity of free will.

Naturally, we cry from the depths of our souls . . . "But God, how could you let something of this magnitude happen?"

How would we want God to act? Do we want him to control the actions of people? In the case of dealing with a terrorist attack, what could possibly be an acceptable number of deaths for God to allow?! Would we feel better if God allowed only the murder of hundreds? Would we rather God allowed only the death of one person? Yet if God would prevent the murder of even one person, there is no longer freedom to choose. People choose to ignore God, to defy God, to go their own way and commit horrible acts against others.

Tragedy, Disaster, Terrorist Attacks: Our World

This planet is not a safe place. Someone might shoot us. Or we might be hit by a car. Or we might have to jump from a building attacked by terrorists. Or any number of things might happen to us in this harsh environment called Earth, the place where God's will is not always followed.

Yet, God is not at the mercy of people, but the other way around. We are at his mercy, fortunately. This is God who created the universe with its uncountable stars, simply by speaking the words, "Let there be lights in the expanse of the sky."[8] This is God who says he "reigns over the nations."[9] He is unlimited in power and wisdom. Though problems seem insurmountable to us, we have an incredibly capable God who reminds us, "Behold, I am the Lord, the God of all flesh; is anything too hard for Me?"[10] Somehow he is able to maintain the freedom of sinful humans, yet still bring about his will. God clearly says, "My counsel shall stand, and I will do all My pleasure."[11] And we can draw comfort from that if our lives are submitted to him. "God opposes the proud, but gives grace to the humble."[12]

Fears, Tragedy, Disaster: Where Is God Now?

Many of us—no, all of us—choose at times to stiff-arm God and his ways. Compared to others, certainly compared to a murderer, we might consider ourselves to be respectable, loving people. But in the raw honesty of our own hearts, if we were to face God, it would be with the knowledge of our sin. As we begin to address God in prayer, are we not caught short, paused by the sense that God is well aware of our thoughts, actions, and self-centeredness? We have . . . by our lives and actions . . . distanced ourselves from God. We have often lived like we could run our lives just fine without him. The Bible says that "We all, like sheep, have gone astray, each of us has turned to his own way."[13]

The consequences? Our sin has separated us from God, and it affects more than this life. The penalty for our sin is death, or eternal separation from God. However, God has provided a way for us to be forgiven and know him.

Inner Strength Through God's Love

God came to Earth to rescue us. "For God so loved the world, that He gave His only begotten Son, that whoever believes in Him should not perish, but have eternal life. For God did not send the Son into the world to judge the world, but that the world should be saved through Him."[14]

God knows the pain and suffering we encounter in

this world. Jesus left the safety and security of his home, and entered the hard environment we live in. Jesus got tired, knew hunger and thirst, battled accusations from others, and was ostracized by family and friends. But Jesus experienced far more than daily hardships. Jesus, the Son of God in human form, willingly took all of our sin on himself and paid our penalty of death. "By this we know love, because He laid down His life for us."[15] He went through torture, dying a slow, humiliating death of suffocation on a cross, so that we could be forgiven.

Jesus told others ahead of time that he would be crucified. He said that three days after his death he would come back to life, proving that he is God. He didn't say he would reincarnate someday. (Who would know if he actually did it?) He said three days after being buried he would show himself physically alive to those who saw his crucifixion. On that third day, Jesus' tomb was found empty and many people testified to seeing him alive.

He now offers us eternal life. We don't earn this. It is a gift from God offered to us, which we receive when we ask him to enter our lives. "The gift of God is eternal life in Christ Jesus."[16] If we repent of our sin and turn back to God, we can have the gift of eternal life through Jesus Christ. It's pretty simple. "God has given us eternal life, and this life is in his Son. He who has the Son has life;

he who does not have the Son of God does not have life."[17] He wants to enter our lives.

Inner Strength Through God's Plan

What about heaven? The Bible says that God has "set eternity in the hearts of men."[18] Maybe that means we know, in our hearts, what a better world would look like. The death of people we love convinces us that there's something very wrong with this life and this world. Somewhere deep down in our souls, we know that there must be a much better place to live, free from heart-wrenching difficulties and pain. To be sure, God does have a better place he offers us. It will be a completely different system in which his will is done all the time. In this world, God will wipe every tear from people's eyes. There will be no more mourning, crying, death, or pain.[19] And God, by his Spirit, will dwell in people in such a way that they will never sin again.[20]

The events of tragedies, disasters, and mass murders are horrific enough. Refusing an eternal relationship with God, which Jesus offers you, would be worse. Not just in light of eternal life, but there is no relationship which compares to knowing God in this life. He is our purpose in life, our source of comfort, our wisdom in confusing times, our strength and hope. "Taste and see that the Lord is good; blessed is the man who takes refuge in him."[21]

It has been said by some that God is just a crutch. But it is likely that he is the only reliable one.

Jesus said, "Peace I leave with you; My peace I give to you; not as the world gives do I give to you. Let not your heart be troubled, neither let it be afraid."[22] For those who will rely on Jesus during their lives, he says it is like building your life on a Rock. Whatever crises attack you in this life, he can keep you strong.

Inner Strength Through God's Son

You can receive Jesus into your life right now. "To all who received him, to those who believed in his name, he gave the right to become children of God."[23] It is through Jesus Christ that we can come back to God. Jesus said, "I am the way, and the truth, and the life; no one comes to the Father, but through Me."[24] Jesus offered, "Behold, I stand at the door and knock; if anyone hears My voice and opens the door, I will come in to him."[25]

Right now you can ask God to enter your life. You can do this through prayer. Prayer means talking honestly with God. At this moment you can call out to God by telling him something like this in sincerity:

> *God, I have turned away from you in my heart, but I want to change that. I want to know you. I want to receive Jesus Christ and his forgiveness into my life. I don't want to be separated from you anymore. Be the God of my life from this day onward. Thank you God.*

Have you just now sincerely asked God into your life? If you have, you have a lot to look forward to. God promises to make your present life one of greater satisfaction through knowing him.[26] Where is God? He promises to make his home in you.[27] And he gives you eternal life.[28]

No matter what happens in the world around you, God can be there for you. Though people do not follow God's ways, God is able to take horrible circumstances and bring about his plan anyway. God is ultimately in control over world events. If you are God's, then you can rest on the promise that "God causes all things to work together for good to those who love God, to those who are called according to His purpose."[29]

Jesus Christ said, "My peace I give to you; not as the world gives do I give to you. Let not your heart be troubled.

In the world you have tribulation, but take courage; I have overcome the world."[30] He promises never to fail us or forsake us.[31]

To grow in your knowledge of God and his will for your life, read the sections Matthew, Mark, Luke, and John in the Bible.

[1] Isaiah 46:9

[2] Psalm 46:1

[3] Jeremiah 29:13

[4] 2 Corinthians 4:8–9

[5] Nahum 1:7

[6] Psalm 145:18–19

[7] Matthew 10:29–31

[8] Genesis 1:14

[9] Psalm 47:8

[10] Jeremiah 32:27

[11] Isaiah 46:10

[12] James 4:6

[13] Isaiah 53:6

[14] John 3:16–17

[15] 1 John 3:16

[16] Romans 6:23

[17] 1 John 5:12

[18] Ecclesiastes 3:11

[19] Revelation 21:4

[20] Revelation 21:27;
     1 Corinthians 15:28

[21] Psalm 34:8

[22] John 14:27

[23] John 1:12

[24] John 14:6

[25] Revelation 3:20

[26] John 10:10

[27] John 14:23

[28] 1 John 5:11–13

[29] Romans 8:28

[30] John 14:27 and 16:33

[31] Hebrews 13:5

For more information about knowing God personally or about the Campus Ministry of Campus Crusade for Christ, visit www.CampusCrusadeforChrist.com. For information about all the ministries of Campus Crusade for Christ, visit www.CCCI.org, or contact: Campus Crusade for Christ, 100 Lake Hart Drive, Orlando, Florida 32832; 407-826-2000.

TEARS AND FEARS
WORKING THROUGH GRIEF
AND TRAUMA

Dr. Helen B. McIntosh

Perhaps in your time of crisis you're wondering: *What do I do now? How do I get past the tears? How do I move past feeling frozen? Why do I feel so sad? How can I stop the memory? Why am I so angry? Will life ever be okay again?* A host of other thoughts and emotions may be flooding your mind and heart, and that's perfectly normal.

The messages you tell yourself and others do matter. These messages can either help or hurt. As you walk through your personal journey of trauma and grief or help others with their healing journey, it helps to follow some simple steps.

If you've ever had a pet die, you may have heard someone say, "Oh, you can get another one." Or, when a grandparent dies, you may have heard, "Well, we can't be sad because she is in a better place." While these comments might be true, the poor timing and insensitivity evoke a deeper hurt.

When tragedy or loss strikes, concerned individuals often don't know what to say or do to help. If we are the one hurting, we may be stuck in how to communicate our needs. In times like this, "just listening" is one of the most therapeutic agents. The following material presents help for processing trauma and grief for both you and others. These suggestions are not exhaustive, but are effective steps in beginning the healing process.

Helping Others with Grief

Grief, which is about *loss* and *change*, happens almost every day for all of us: children of all ages and adults. We may lose a parent, a child, a grandparent, a friend, or a pet. Or we may grieve over the loss of relationship through divorce, a move, a change in someone's health, or a change of schools. Sometimes, we may suffer a traumatic loss of a number of people at once, like the friends, roommates, professors, and colleagues lost in the Virginia Tech massacre.

The loss of even *one* person is profound, but when there are multiple losses, the tears and grief magnify.

Many think that young people are emotionally adaptable, that they can get over grief relatively quickly. But evidence shows that losses experienced in youth that are not adequately worked through cause great scars and pain further into adulthood. The following information serves as a guide to help the grieving cope with their losses and changes, and assist those who minister to the hurting.

If you are coming alongside a grieving individual, your own grief process is extremely important, too. It is crucial that you are processing these same steps and getting the help you need as well.

1. **Build the relationship.** Spend some time helping the individual to feel comfortable with you. In counseling terms, it's called "being with" and is the involvement or connecting element. This is even more important than "having all the answers."

Examples: "I know you are hurting . . . this is a tough time for you . . . I'd like to help you . . . could we talk?"

Be aware that the way you say things is just as important as what you say. Be slow and gentle with your words and tone of voice.

2. **Listen to the person's story.** Listening to a grieving person's story and validating his or her pain are important pieces of the healing process. Your purpose is to get the hurting individual to talk, to share, and to "un-stuff." You may want to say, "Maybe you could share what you're thinking right now. Could you tell me about (the trauma, the person, the friend)? Tell me some things about this friend. . . ."

3. **Affirm the relationship.** If the person begins to talk, let him or her do so without interruption. Some prompts for you to use to stimulate discussion include:

"(The person or friend) was so lucky to have you for a friend (or brother, sister, classmate). I can see you cared a lot for (the person, friend). . . ."

"I'll bet you were a gift to (the person, friend). He/she was lucky or blessed to have you care about him/her so much. I can see you meant a lot to each other."

4. **Share best memories.** Many times we can help a grieving person "remember" as well as honor a lost loved one(s) by helping the person create something or even planting something in the loved one's memory.

Encourage the individual to share his or her best memories as you say something like, "What are some of your best memories of (the person)? Tell me about them if that's okay. Do you want to share a memory, write a poem, create a scrapbook, or plant a memorial tree?"

5. **Give some feedback.**

First, ask if you can give some feedback:

- "May I share some thoughts with you?"

If you get a positive response, you may want to say something like:

- "We are all different and will respond differently."

- "It's okay to cry (you've had something very sad happen), and it's okay if you don't cry. Sometimes we feel numb (nothing) when something sad happens. People process or think through their sad times differently."

- "It's okay to remember—and it's okay to forget."
  - "Ways we remember (the person) is to talk about the good times and special memories. Sometimes it helps to write these special memories down or even to draw them."
  - "Would you like to make a card for (the person)'s family or another person who hurts as much as you do?"

• "There will be a lot of times today you will not remember (the person). You will be eating lunch or resting or many other things. Then when you remember the hurt, you might feel bad or guilty that you weren't thinking about the loss. But I want you to know that it's normal and it's okay. The person [who died] would want you to live life fully and to do the things you used to do."

• "It's okay to share your feelings."
  • "Would you feel safe enough to share what you are feeling right now?"
  • "At a later time when you are feeling sad or scared, it's okay for you to just say to me, 'I feel sad and need to share,' or 'I feel sad and need a hug.'"

• "It will hurt for many days but it will get better."
  • "My/our job is to listen and yours is to share when you feel you want to as you keep remembering."

• "It's okay that you survived even though your friend died. He/she would want you to celebrate and treasure life when you can. . . ." [Feeling guilt after someone dies is very common and is called "survivor's guilt." See the next section on "reframing" to further explore processing this reaction.]

6. **Talk about attending the funeral.** A funeral can bring closure because the mourner sees the reality of the death. But it can also be a difficult experience for some. You might want to talk to the individual and encourage him/her to tell how he/she feels about going to the funeral. Ask what the person wants and doesn't want, and what he or she feels comfortable doing or doesn't feel comfortable doing. A creative alternative could be to go to the funeral but not view the body.

7. **Avoid saying certain clichés to the grieving.** "He's better off . . ." or "I know how you feel . . ." or "Time will take care of it. . . ."

Better choices are: "I am so sad. . . ." "I hurt with you. . . ." or "I don't know what to say. . . ."

8. **Ask, "Do you have any questions about this?"** This is the grieving person's time to ask you specifics. Answer what you can, but if you are uncomfortable answering anything, tell the individual you want to think about it some more before you answer. Be honest if you don't know

the answer. Get help yourself if you need it! If the person has questions about death, eternity, or other spiritual matters, assure the person that you will find help for him or her to better understand what has happened.

9. **Celebrate life when it is time.** After you talk to the grieving individual about the loss or change—if it seems natural or feels right—do something special with the person. Some examples are taking a walk, reading a book, having coffee, or even entering an established routine as a way of saying, "It's okay to celebrate life . . . it's okay to go back to a routine right now."

10. **Compile verses for a grief notebook.** It is very helpful to create a notebook for someone going through this "valley of the shadow." Often sharing hope-filled verses from God's Word is a tremendous encouragement. We don't want to ever communicate to someone, "Take two verses and call me in the morning," by treating verses as a "stick on" that become rote. God's written words are treasures not to be shared out of season. But by placing these verses in a notebook, you are providing a rich resource for the hurting one(s) to reach for in God's perfect timing. Examples of faith promises (from the New American Standard Version) are:

Psalm 23:4 "Even though I walk through the valley of the shadow of death, I fear no evil, for You are with me; Your rod and Your staff, they comfort me."

Psalm 34:1, 17–19 "I will bless the Lord at all times; His praise shall continually be in my mouth. The righteous cry, and the Lord hears and delivers them out of all their troubles. The Lord is near to the brokenhearted and saves those who are crushed in spirit. Many are the afflictions of the righteous, but the Lord delivers him out of them all."

Isaiah 61:2–3 ". . . To comfort all who mourn, to grant those who mourn in Zion, giving them a garland instead of ashes, the oil of gladness instead of mourning, the mantle of praise instead of a spirit of fainting [heaviness]. So they will be called oaks of righteousness, the planting of the Lord, that He may be glorified."

Other References to Use for Such a Notebook Include:

2 Samuel 12:23	Psalm 42:3, 8
Job 1:21–22	Psalm 116:15
Psalm 56:8	Psalm 119:18, 25
Psalm 40	Psalm 139:6

Psalm 147:3

Proverbs 3:5–6

Isaiah 40:8, 27–31

Isaiah 57:1–2

Jeremiah 31:13

Jeremiah 33:3

Habakkuk 3:17–19

Matthew 5:4

Luke 20:36

John 10:28

John 14:2

John 17:24

Romans 8:18

Romans 8:28, 35–39

1 Corinthians 13:12

2 Corinthians 1:3–5, 7

2 Corinthians 4:17–18

2 Corinthians 5:8

2 Corinthians 7:6–7

2 Corinthians 9:8

Ephesians 3:14–15, 16

Philippians 1:21

Philippians 4:8–9

1 Thessalonians 4:17–18

2 Thessalonians 2:15–17

Hebrews 4:9

Hebrews 11:13–16

James 5:10–11

1 Peter 1:3–4

Revelation 21:4

Revelation 22:4

The death of a loved one or even an acquaintance is a teachable time and opens many opportunities to share the plan of salvation as well as the promises of eternal life. Young people in particular face not only losses and changes, but also anxiety about the things that they don't understand. If they are encouraged to ask questions, there is less of an opportunity for the anxiety of the unknown. It is also okay for young adults to see you grieve over the losses and changes in your own life and to see God's grace envelop you. Share with them how God is helping you. In these conversations, there is mutual encouragement as you both share verses that have ministered to your own hearts.

Helping Others Process Trauma

Life is hard. Even on a rare day that seems "hassle-free," most of us have many weighty situations on our hearts. Sometimes it feels too much for our hearts to bear. What do we do with it all? How do we continue to function even though there is great heaviness around us? Is there a way we can process all of the heaviness and keep our hearts strong? What if there is a truly terrible event from our past that we can't forget? What if we witnessed a campus shooting? How can our hearts and memories heal?

In looking at the effects of exposure to a trauma or crisis, it's important to realize that fears differ from anxiety in that they are more specific. Anxiety is that looming dark cloud that defies a label. God longs to sweep away the cloud and to bring your anxious thoughts out of the dark. He wants to bring you to complete recovery.

You may be familiar with the term post-traumatic stress disorder (PTSD). PTSD can occur after one is exposed to a frightening event where there is real or perceived danger present, affecting you beyond the normal range of reactions. Even family members or others not directly involved are also at risk for PTSD because of the trauma they also feel and cannot "shake."

Common symptoms of PTSD include:

- Continually reliving the event or having flashbacks
- A hypersensitivity to various things connected to the "memory" (a smell or sound)
- Ongoing depression, dissociation, memory loss, and other ways of avoiding "remembering"
- Marked changes in one's interests, emotions, sleep patterns, concentration, and ability to relax

An effective option for healing from the symptoms of PTSD is based on cognitive-behavioral therapy, which is the belief that what one is thinking directly affects one's choices. Or, another way of saying it is that "what one thinks will determine one's behavior."

One simple method that I have used for more than thirty years with great success is a method of "reframing" the trauma or traumatic memory when it surfaces until it diminishes.

Reframing is not "positive thinking" or trying to cheer yourself up. It is not about dismissing or diminishing your legitimate pain and it's not about masking your true feelings. Reframing is not a quick fix, and although it will become a habit it is not a mechanical ritual you perform with a fake smile plastered on your face.

So what is reframing?

How to "Reframe" PTSD

Reframing is an exercise. It's a way to train your brain and therefore your heart. It's a choice you make and one you'll need to choose to make diligently as anxious and weighty thoughts surface.

The first step is to record your thinking. Yes, your thinking may be dark and flawed, but is important information.

Record your thought(s) or memory (memories) in the left-hand column of the Truth Chart that follows this section. You may want to begin with words like, "I feel so scared. . . ." or "I am remembering. . . ." or "I am thinking about the bad memory again. . . ." Try not to edit what you are writing. Avoid blaming/shaming and should/shouldn't messages such as, "I shouldn't feel this way. . . ."

An anchor verse for this column is 2 Corinthians 10:3–5 (NASB):

"For though we walk in the flesh, we do not war according to the flesh, for the weapons of our warfare are not of the flesh, but divinely powerful for the destruction of fortresses. We are destroying speculations and every lofty thing raised up against the knowledge of God, and we are taking every thought captive to the obedience of Christ."

Use the left-hand column to name your stronghold—that unhealthy place where injury or trauma and memory continues to play. It's a worn path, a place that has refused to be comforted. It is often a secret place in your thinking and in your heart. Those are the "speculations" mentioned in 2 Corinthians 10:5. For your healing, these feelings/thoughts must be compared to and lined up with what God says, and your lies must be thrown out. That's when the strongholds fall.

Only God can liberate us, freeing us from destructive patterns that have been in our thought life over a period of time. We are going to ask God to let us see our trauma and bad memory from *his* point of view. We are going to learn to be good listeners and then to record what we feel that God is saying about our situation . . . and then camp there. We will not have healing from our trauma if we stay in the left-hand column. The anchor verse for the right-hand column is John 8:31–32 (NASB).

"If you abide in My word, you are My disciples indeed. And you shall know the truth, and the truth shall make you free."

As these "true" statements come to mind, write them down in the right-hand column opposite the thinking and feeling statement(s). Most important, every time you are bombarded with thoughts and feelings from the left-hand column, say out loud, "The truth is. . . ." and share one of your truths from that right-hand column. This is where you are to stand and to stay! The peace and rest comes when you can see things from God's perspective. Then, and only then, truth liberates you.

THINKING 2 Corinthians 10:3–5	TRUTH John 8:31–32
I feel so scared . . . I don't feel safe . . .	But the truth is . . . it is normal right now for me to feel unsettled. I have been through so much. Grief and anxiety have gotten all tangled up and I feel like a mess. I feel the Lord is giving me permission to cry and to rest. But, God, you are enough for this nightmare. You are my Safety. You are my Comfort. I choose right now to trust you and I will choose *not* to camp my thoughts on the memories of what happened. I have honored those lost, and it is okay for me to move my thoughts to a more whole place to heal my heart now. I thank you for the promise in Matthew 11:28–30 that I am yoked together with you. I am weary and heavy-laden and you will give me rest for my soul.

THINKING 2 Corinthians 10:3–5	TRUTH John 8:31–32
I am thinking about the bad memory again . . .	Lord, what is it that you want to tell me and show me? I invite you into my memory now. What are you saying to me? If there is something from the bad memory that I am to learn, let me know that now. If not—I am going to choose to change channels. I am going to focus on you as many times today as I "remember." Lord, I thank you for healing me more each day and strengthening me. Thank you for the feeling of compassion that has arisen from this. May I see the other strengths you have given me during this dark season of my life? . . .
I feel badly having survived and my friend didn't survive . . .	But the truth is, this is my reality. It is called "survivor's guilt" and my friend would not want me to feel this false guilt. This action wasn't my fault. My friend would want me to live life fully

THINKING 2 Corinthians 10:3–5	TRUTH John 8:31–32
	with no regrets. What I am feeling is really common. It is okay to ask for help. God, please show me in the secret place of my heart what your thoughts are toward me, and encourage me with your plan for my life. I know you are enough for this dark place in my life . . .
I actually *don't* feel . . .	But the truth is, this happens to a lot of people. My heart can't take care of the enormity of my grief, so it is buried beneath the ice. Lord, help me to see this from your perspective. Help me to see that this valley of the shadow is only a chapter in my life but isn't the whole story. Who might you want me to begin to tell my story to—that would be safe for me emotionally—that when the time is right, the layers will come off? The

THINKING 2 Corinthians 10:3–5	TRUTH John 8:31–32
	frozenness is a self-protection layer for me to bear the pain of it all, but I know it is dangerous to stuff my pain too long. Help me, Lord. Send comfort to my head and heart . . .
Why didn't God take me instead? . . .	But the truth is, I will never know until heaven (that's when I can ask you, Lord)—but *by faith* I choose to stand on the belief that there is a plan for my life. Lord, you alone know the answer. You alone know the numbers of hairs on my head. You alone know the length of my days on Earth. You alone know what is best for me. I rest in your plan for my life, even if I don't understand. I rest in your sovereignty . . .
I feel overwhelmed and depressed. . . .	But the truth is, what I have been through *is* overwhelming. My emo-

THINKING 2 Corinthians 10:3–5	TRUTH John 8:31–32
	tions are exhausted and depleted. That's why I feel depressed. But, the truth is, I don't have to stay in this condition. I can take every detail to you, Lord, and ask for clarity and then ask for grace over it. If I resist your grace, I could even become bitter (Hebrews 12:15). You want me well. I am asking for your grace . . .
I just want to escape from all this forever . . .	But the truth is, it is natural and normal to want to escape this forever. But, Lord, you have fully equipped your children for battle. You have said that in this world we will have tribulation and hardship. It feels almost too hard, but I choose right now to go deeper in you; for as I abide in you, I shall be given all I need to recover from all this . . .

THINKING 2 Corinthians 10:3–5	TRUTH John 8:31–32
I'm afraid if I talk about my pain, it will be too much for me to handle . . .	But the truth is, God is longing for me to talk to him about this so it *isn't* too much. It's not healthy to stuff the memory and not to speak of it. Jesus asked a man at the pool called Bethesda (who had been in his sickness for thirty-eight years), "Do you wish to get well?" That's my question, too. If I really want to get well, I will talk to God and talk to others (who are helpful and safe) until my heart is at peace. Lord, will you help me to take a first step? . . .
I can't sleep. My mind just keeps racing . . .	But the truth is, there are three things I can do. One is to seek my doctor's advice about possible and temporary medication to get me sleeping again. Second, the "racing" is the battle in my mind. I have complete control over which "channel" I'm on and stay on. I can choose to

THINKING 2 Corinthians 10:3–5	TRUTH John 8:31–32
	focus on God or the bad memory. It is my choice. I hold the remote control! Last, but best of all—I can seek God in the night. I can ask him to speak to me. I can praise him. I can be an intercessor for others. I can worship . . .
I'm afraid to really cry about all of it. I'm afraid if I start, I won't stop.	But the truth is, it is really okay to cry. That is my heart "leaking." Even Jesus wept. Even if I didn't stop crying for hours initially, my body will know when it is time to stop and rest from it. If there are additional seasons of tears, that's okay, too. The opposite of crying is far more damaging—to stuff the grief. I can ask God to help me to cry as he wishes me to, to unleash, to feel, and to receive his grace and peace at the end. This season of grief is preparing me for the years ahead. Life is hard

THINKING 2 Corinthians 10:3–5	TRUTH John 8:31–32
	and full of trouble. I can learn right now how to grieve well.
What if I don't feel like God is there anymore? ...	But the truth is, he is there. I may not *feel* like it, but Scripture promises that he is always there for me and hears my cry. The truth is, my fear of processing what has happened is actually preventing my healing. My fear has shut down my feelings. Lord, help me to connect with you as I once did. How did I leave the path? Was it choosing to fear and not to trust you? Show me the path back ...

THINKING	TRUTH

THINKING	TRUTH

Do you sense the battle for your mind and heart? Do you also sense God's strength and purpose to comfort you? I trust you did not hear a "quick fix" in these examples but that you heard an ongoing dialogue with the Lord of the universe who wants you to trust him and see your hard place from his point of view. It is choosing to "camp out" on the right-hand column where the victory and freedom are.

Ask him to help you learn to listen more and more. He is speaking to you in countless ways through that "still small voice," verses, praise music, quiet walks, others, and even various circumstances. Be assured that he is *longing* to answer your cry. *Longing* to lift you up. *Longing* to experience new intimacy and fellowship with you as you turn to him for comfort. He is *longing* to heal your heart and memories.

©2007 Dr. Helen B. McIntosh

Dr. Helen B. McIntosh, wife, mother, grandmother, speaker, author, and inventor of The Peace Rug, has a passion for helping kids and adults with restoration. Her children's book is entitled *Eric, Jose & The Peace Rug* (2007), and her adult book is entitled *Extreme Damage Makeover from the Inside Out* (2007). A licensed professional counselor (LPC) and certified in Reality Therapy (RTC), Dr. McIntosh has spent more than eighteen years in public education, twelve as school counselor at Roan School in Dalton,

Georgia. She has a B.A. in psychology from Hollins College in Virginia; a master's degree in guidance and counseling from West Georgia College; a specialist degree in guidance and counseling from the State University of West Georgia; and a doctorate in counseling psychology from the University of Sarasota. Dr. McIntosh lives in Dalton, Georgia with her family. Her website is www.peacerug.com

NOTES

Chapter 1   No Words

1. Trey Perkins, "Horror at Virginia Tech: A Sorrow Beyond Words," *People*, April 30, 2007, p. 59.

2. Blacksburg weather conditions, April 16, 2007, www.wunderground.com/history.

3. David Maraniss, "That Was the Desk I Chose to Die Under," WashingtonPost.com, April 19, 2007, http://www.washingtonpost.com/wpdyn/content/article/2007/04/18/AR2007041802824_pf.html.

4. Molly Donohue, telephone interview, May 2007.

5. Evan Thomas, "Making of a Massacre," *Newsweek*, April 30, 2007, p. 29.

6. "Freshman Who Found Students Dead Believes Cho Should Be Forgiven," *Good Morning America*, ABCnews.com, April 19, 2007, http://abcnews.go.com/GMA/VATech/Story?id=3055979&page=2.

7. Tim Thornton, "All I was doing was saying, 'What can I do? What can I do to help?'" *The Roanoke Times*, May 19, 2007, http://www.roanoke.com/vtcampus/wb/117425.

8. Associated Press, "Virginia Tech Gunman Was 'Well-Prepared' to Extend Shooting Spree With More Than 200 Extra Rounds,"

241

Foxnews.com, May 21, 2007, http://www.foxnews.com/story/0,2933,274492,00.html.

9. Seung-Hui Cho manifesto package, April 16, 2007, http://www.msnbc.msn.com/id/18186053/ and http://www.11alive.com/news/article_news.aspx?storyid=95628&provider=top.

10. Haiyan Cheng, in-person interview, April 2007.

11. John Riley, "Cho's Rage," *Newsday*, reprinted in *The Gazette,* Colorado Springs, Colorado, April 19, 2007.

Chapter 2   "Please Call."

1. Julie Harrison, telephone interview, May 2007.

2. Lisa Highfield, in-person interview, May 2007.

3. Dana Cox, in-person interview, May 2007.

4. Molly Donohue, telephone interview, May 2007.

5. Lauren McCain's page, myspace.com, http://profile.myspace.com/index.cfm?fuseaction=user.viewprofile&friendid=14903990.

6. Tim Thornton, "All I was doing was saying, 'What can I do? What can I do to help?'" *The Roanoke Times*, May 19, 2007, http://www.roanoke.com/vtcampus/wb/117425.

7. Dave and Sherry McCain, telephone interview, May 2007.

8. Ruiqi Zhang, telephone interview, May 2007.

9. Jeff Highfield, in-person interview, May 2007.

Chapter 3   Lights in the Darkness

1. Andrew Duggleby, e-mail interview, May 2007.

2. Beth Macy, "Family of engineers," *The Roanoke Times*, May 5, 2007, http://www.roanoke.com/news/roanoke/wb/115727.

3. Lisa Highfield in-person interview, May 2007.

4. Virginia Tech international students statistics, Cranwell Center, http://www.uusa.vt.edu/cranwell/flagpage06.jpg.

5.   Erin Carter, in-person interview, May 2007.

6.   Cynthia Thomas, CRU blog, "How We're Doing," April 17, 2007, http://campuscrusadeforchrist.com/virginiatech/how-were-doing/.

7.   Clay Violand, e-mail interview, May 2007.

8.   Elizabeth Cohen, "Mom: My son was in the room when Cho killed himself," CNN.com, April 20, 2007, http://www.cnn.com/2007/US/04/19/vtech.victims/index.html?eref=rss_topstories.

9.   Tonia Moxley, "Media throng sets up shop in Blacksburg," *The Roanoke Times,* April 18, 2007, http://www.roanoke.com/news/nrv/wb/wb/xp-113606.

10. Sandra Jackson, in-person interview, May 2007.

11. Dana Cox, in-person interview, May 2007.

12. Sherry McCain, telephone interview, May 2007.

13. Julie Harrison, telephone interview, May 2007.

14. Dave McCain, telephone interview, May 2007.

15. President George W. Bush, Virginia Tech Memorial Convocation, April 17, 2007, http://www.whitehouse.gov/news/releases/2007/04/20070417-1.html.

16. Lauren McCain's page, myspace.com, http://profile.myspace.com/index.cfm?fuseaction=user.viewprofile&friendid=14903990.

Chapter 4   The Love of My Life

1.   Sean Mussenden, "Funeral for Mary Read," WSLS News Channel 10, April 25, 2007, http://www.wsls.com/servlet/Satellite?pagename=WSLS%2FMGArticle%2FSLS_BasicArticle&c=MGArticle&cid=1173350939692&path=!news!localnews.

2.   Brandon Overby, in-person interview, May 2007.

3.   Allie Burgin, "My heartache," *New River Valley Magazine*, May–June 2007, Country Media, Inc., Blacksburg, Virginia, pp. 6–8.

4.   Sherry McCain, telephone interview, May 2007.

5. Blair Pippin, in-person interview, May 2007.

6. Dave McCain, telephone interview, May 2007.

7. Amy Yates, telephone interview, May 2007.

8. Chum Hoang, in-person interview, May 2007.

9. Cynthia Thomas, telephone interview, May 2007.

10. Lauren McCain's page, myspace.com, http://profile.myspace.com/index.cfm?fuseaction=user.viewprofile&friendid=14903990.

Chapter 5   "This Stinks. This Hurts."

1. Lisa Finneran, "Hampton woman a Virginia Tech victim," Dailypress.com, April 17, 2007, http://www.dailypress.com/news/local/dp-now-hamptonvic.a17,0,432420.story?page=2&coll=dp-news-local-final.

2. Doreen Tomlin, telephone interview, May 2007.

3. Tony Arnold, in-person and e-mail interviews, April and May, 2007.

4. Lisa Highfield, in-person interview, May 2007.

5. Dr. Helen McIntosh, telephone and e-mail interviews, May 2007.

6. Governor Tim Kaine, Virginia Tech Memorial Convocation, April 17, 2007, http://www.governor.virginia.gov/MediaRelations/Speeches/2007/VT-Convo.cfm.

7. Sherry McCain, telephone interview, May 2007.

8. Jeff Highfield, in-person interview, May 2007.

9. Sassie Duggleby, in-person interview, May 2007.

10. Jim Pace, in-person interview, May 2007.

11. Cynthia Thomas, CRU blog, "When It Rains It Pours," April 20, 2007, http://campuscrusadeforchrist.com/virginiatech/when-it-rains-it-pours/.

12. Andrea Kebede, in-person interview, May 2007.

Chapter 6   I Can Only Imagine

1. Mark Stremler, in-person interview, May 2007.
2. Lauren McCain, video interview, Campus Crusade for Christ, February 22, 2007.
3. Sherry McCain, telephone interview, May 2007.
4. Phillip Zellner, telephone interview, May 2007.
5. Dave McCain, telephone interview, May 2007.
6. Amy Yates, telephone interview, May 2007.
7. Leah Mummert, telephone interview, May 2007.

Chapter 7   Hope for the Helpless

1. Sun-Kyung Cho, "Cho family statement," CNN.com, April 20, 2007, http://www.cnn.com/2007/US/04/20/shooting.family.statement/index.html.
2. Dr. Julie Cox, telephone interview, June 2007.
3. Joe Guthrie, in-person interview, May 2007.
4. Cynthia Thomas, CRU blog, "Cru," April 20, 2007, http://campuscrusadeforchrist.com/virginiatech/category/cynthias-blog/page/2/.

Chapter 8   I Forgive You

1. Corrie ten Boom, *Two Days Longer*, Beth Lueders (Howard Publishing: West Monroe, Louisiana, 2006) pp. 65–66; http://www.hoyweb.com/faq/forgive2.htm.
2. Doreen Tomlin, telephone interview, May 2007.
3. C. S. Lewis, http://www.wildershow.com/cs-lewis-forgive.htm.
4. Molly Donohue, telephone interview, May 2007.
5. William Shakespeare, http://www.worldofquotes.com/topic/Forgiveness/1/index.html.

6. Cynthia Thomas, telephone interview, May 2007.

7. Young-Hwan Kim, telephone interview, May 2007.

8. Hyun "David" Chung, telephone interview, May 2007.

9. Evan Thomas, "Making of a Massacre," *Newsweek*, April 30, 2007, pp. 24, 31.

10. Ian Shapira and Tom Jackman, "Morning of Horror," *The Washington Post*, reprinted in *The Gazette*, Colorado Springs, Colorado, April 17, 2007, p. A1.

11. Bob Jackson, in-person and e-mail interviews, May 2007.

12. Phillip Zellner, telephone interview, May 2007.

13. Lauren McCain, journal entry, August 16, 2007.

14. Dr. Julie Cox, telephone interview, June 2007.

15. Dave McCain, telephone interview, May 2007.

Chapter 9   Circle of Friends

1. Jeff Highfield, in-person interview, May 2007.

2. Phillip Zellner, telephone interview, May 2007.

3. Lisa Highfield, in-person interview, May 2007.

4. Chum Hoang, in-person interview, May 2007.

5. Blair Pippin, in-person interview, May 2007.

6. Sandra Jackson, in-person interview, May 2007.

7. Dave and Sherry McCain, telephone interview, May 2007.

Chapter 10   Dancing Before Him

1. Chum Hoang, in-person interview, May 2007.

2. Molly Donohue, telephone interview, May 2007

3. Karen Macri, telephone interview, May 2007.

4. Julie Harrison, telephone interview, May 2007.

5. R. J. Reel, telephone interview, May 2007.

6.   Dana Cox, in-person interview, May 2007.

7.   Dana Cox, in-person interview, May 2007.

6.   Dave and Sherry McCain, telephone interview, May 2007.

All in-person interviews were conducted by Beth Lueders with additional telephone interviews by Ann Work and Diane McDougall.

Photo by Robert Parham

ABOUT THE AUTHOR

Interrogated by Communist soldiers and threatened at knifepoint while on an overseas assignment, Beth Lueders is an award-winning journalist who adds captivating adventure and intrigue to her writing. She has covered stories in nearly twenty countries for several magazines and newspapers, Beth is the founder and director of MacBeth Communications, a writing and editorial business.

Beth's journalistic work has garnered five Evangelical Press Association Awards, including an award for investigative reporting on the plight of radiation-poisoned Byelorussian children and at-risk prostitutes in the Philippines. Beth is a former staff member of Campus Crusade for

Christ and former editor for *Clarity* and *Worldwide Challenge* magazines.

Beth is also a seminar and retreat speaker and has published hundreds of articles and media pieces for numerous publications and organizations including: Celestial Seasonings; CHEFS; Compassion International; Cook Communications; Current, Inc.; *Discipleship Journal*; Focus on the Family; International Bible Society; *Leadership*; *Moody*; Promise Keepers; and *Reader's Digest*.

She has authored, co-authored, and edited several books including her most recent, *Two Days Longer*, and *Q&A with Point of Grace* and the *Women of Faith Study Bible*. Beth currently resides in Colorado Springs. For more information about Beth or to schedule her for speaking engagements, visit BethLueders.com.